P9-CPZ-718

Merrill C Davis

FAITH AND NURTURE

FAITH
AND
NURTURE

BY

H. SHELTON SMITH

NEW YORK

CHARLES SCRIBNER'S SONS

1941

To

A. B. S.

PREFACE

THAT the modern movement in Protestant religious education is confronted with a crucial decision in its theological orientation can hardly be denied. The necessity for making a decisive choice derives from the emergence of post-liberal patterns of religious thought which now challenge the central assumptions and concepts of liberal Christian nurture. The question therefore has arisen: Shall Protestant nurture realign its theological foundations with the newer currents of Christian thought, or shall it resist those currents and merely reaffirm its faith in traditional liberalism?

The latter alternative appears to be the choice that is being made by some of the most prominent leaders in Protestant nurture. With that choice, however, I find myself compelled to disagree, even though I deeply respect those who have made it. It seems to me that the thought-patterns of modern liberal religious nurture have largely exhausted their vitality, and that failure to reconstruct them in terms of a more adequate faith will ultimately result in the collapse, or at least the slow death, of the twentieth-century movement of religious education.

In what more important respects the theological framework of liberal Protestant nurture calls for reconsideration and revision this book attempts to show. There is no attempt to deal with the entire philosophy of current religious education. Our purpose, rather, is to raise into sharp relief certain basic aspects of Christian faith which seem either to be ignored or else inadequately incorporated in the modern theory of liberal religious nurture. The central emphases of liberal faith are considered in their broad cultural contexts, and in terms of their long-time historic trends. Only from this perspective, it is believed, may one adequately comprehend the wider significance of the contemporary faith of Protestant nurture.

Viewed in historical perspective, present-day nurture is essentially the child of the religious faith of the late nineteenth century. Its most characteristic theological ideas had attained cultural maturity in American Protestantism before the advent of the first World War. Able and significant books, to be sure, have been written since that time; nevertheless, their basic theological framework was fashioned by the culture of the pre-War era. This fact will explain why this volume lays so much emphasis on the earlier works in Protestant educational philosophy.

While this book attempts to show the need for the revision of the thought-patterns of liberal Protestant nurture, it also recognizes that the newer currents of theological thought are themselves defective in certain respects. The immediate task of the Christian educator, as it seems to the present writer, is neither iconoclastic rejection of religious liberalism, nor the adoption *en bloc* of what is called realistic theology. What seems to be desired, rather, is penetrating and persistent criticism applied to both modes of thought, combined with a willingness to learn from exponents of either point of view.

On first glance this volume will doubtless seem to some to reflect primarily a negative attitude, since it devotes a considerable amount of space to the analysis and critical evaluation of the assumptions, concepts, and tendencies of liberal faith. If, however, one follows the argument of the book as a whole it will be seen to focus attention not only upon elements of weakness in religious liberalism, but also upon lines of constructive advance. If the reader finds it falling somewhat short on the side of construction it is hoped that he will remember that every past effort to find a way forward in Christian thinking has been characterized, at least in its earlier phase, less by constructive achievement than by critical reconsideration. So far as liberal Protestant nurture is concerned, the writer believes that the present situation calls less for construction than for unsparing criticism. For until religious educators recognize more fully the grave limitations of the underlying theology of liberal nurture there can be little hope of any serious effort at positive reconstruction.

In both content and form this book is indebted to many different persons and groups. Of the latter, I must mention in particular those student-groups who have composed my classes and seminars during the past decade. By unflinching criticism of unconventional views and by unfailing manifestations of goodwill, by healthy skepticism and by undeserved confidence, they have helped to germinate and mature many of the ideas that are here offered the reader.

Of the former, I cannot hope to include, save in spirit, all those individual friends who have directly or indirectly shared in the shaping of the thought of these chapters. I must, however, specify certain of those who have been of more immediate assistance. To Reinhold Niebuhr I owe a twofold debt. For more than a decade I, like many others, have found his thought a well-spring of ethical and religious creativity; and this was all I really had any right to ask of him. Nevertheless, he graciously read my entire manuscript and made a number of very valuable suggestions. Of my colleagues in Duke University, Professor B. Harvie Branscomb and Professor Albert C. Outler generously gave me much-needed help. Professor Branscomb read certain portions of the manuscript and made suggestions which served to clarify my thought at several important points. To Professor Outler, however, I am in the heaviest debt of all. At two different stages he read with critical and painstaking care the entire manuscript, and gave me invaluable assistance.

In addition to those already mentioned, I wish to thank my secretary, Miss Thelma Hubbard, who patiently retyped the manuscript in its various versions; and Mr. John B. Bennett, Gurney Harriss Kearns Fellow in Religion in Duke University, who verified all the footnote references and assisted in the preparation of the index. The friendly and competent service of Mr. W. L. Savage and his associates of Charles Scribner's Sons made it a pleasant task to bring this volume to publication. My wife, Alma Bowden Smith, would be the last person to admit that she had made any contribution to this book; nevertheless, I here gratefully acknowledge that she has been of incalculable assistance at every stage.

To those who may wish the help of a bibliography, may I suggest that they will find rather detailed guidance in the footnotes of the various chapters.

H. SHELTON SMITH

Duke University
Durham, North Carolina
June, 1941

CONTENTS

FAITH AND NURTURE

CHAPTER ONE

LIBERAL FAITH AND
PROTESTANT NURTURE

THE FIRST two decades of the present century witnessed the emergence of religious education as one of the major movements of American Protestantism.[1] With the advent of the century, this movement gained the active support of many of Protestantism's most prominent leaders in religious and educational thought. Shortly after the first World War the idea of a "teaching church" swept through the country with almost irresistible force. From the standpoint of popular interest religious education eclipsed perhaps every other project of the churches. Large numbers of men and women sought specialized training for service in its ranks.[2]

Like every other complex movement, this educational awakening in the churches was the result of many different factors. Among those factors must be included new developments in sociology, psychology, and educational philosophy. Any complete analysis, however, must reveal the fact that it was in no small measure the fruit of a new mode of reli-

[1]See H. F. Cope, "Twenty Years' Progress in Religious Education," *Religious Education,* XVIII (1923), pp. 307–316.
[2]In Boston University School of Religious Education, for example, the enrollment increased from 105 in 1918 to 607 in 1928. Walter S. Athearn, *An Adventure in Religious Education* (New York, 1930), p. 47.

gious life and thought. This new outlook, which we shall presently outline in terms of its dominant tendencies of thought, is usually called liberal Christianity.[3]

As we shall see, liberalism was a vital element in American Protestant thought long before the rise of twentieth-century religious education. In view of Horace Bushnell's epoch-making book on *Christian Nurture* in the middle of the nineteenth century, it is rather surprising that the teaching activities of the Church should have remained so largely unresponsive to liberal modes of theological thought. With the advent of the present century, however, Christian liberalism became an influential factor in the educational theory of the Protestant churches.

1. The Crisis of Liberal Religious Education

AFTER AN ERA of advance, liberal religious education now finds itself on the defensive. Indeed, from the standpoint of underlying philosophy, it is passing through a period of deepening crisis. The basic factor in this crisis arises from the fact that the mode of religious thought in which liberal nurture is rooted is now undergoing searching criticism and fundamental reconstruction.[1] One of our younger theologians has recently written: "Liberalism as a religious move-

---

[3]It is also frequently referred to as "progressive" or "modern" Christianity. None of these terms, however, carries a very definite meaning. For this reason, we have chosen to identify liberalism in terms of certain broad historic tendencies in American Protestantism.

[1]See, for example, John C. Bennett, "After Liberalism—What?" *Christian Century,* L (1933), pp. 1403–1406; Harry Emerson Fosdick, "Beyond Modernism," *Christian Century,* LII (1935), pp. 1549–1552; Reinhold Niebuhr, *Moral Man and Immoral Society* (New York, 1932); Walter M. Horton, *Realistic Theology* (New York, 1936), Chap. 1; Reinhold Niebuhr, "Ten Years that Shook My World," *Christian Century,* LVI (1939), pp. 542–546.

ment seems to have failed."[2] This is the verdict of many leaders of current religious thought.

It is significant, however, that this criticism of liberalism has found little sympathy among religious educators. They are sharply critical of the critics, and for the most part they simply reiterate the characteristic tenets of liberal religion.[3] It is not uncommon for these defenders of liberal orthodoxy to lump together all those who oppose them and describe the entire group as "Barthian" or "neo-orthodox." Many of them vigorously dissent from the underlying religious viewpoint of the recent ecumenical conferences. Thus George A. Coe writes: "Oxford puts religious 'education' in peril."[4] Criticisms of a similar sort are being expressed by other well-known religious educators.[5]

This tendency of the religious educator merely to reaffirm the faith of liberalism, combined with only a negative reaction to the newer currents of Christian thought, gives little promise of revitalizing the educational movement of the Protestant churches. There is an important element of truth in Shailer Mathews' statement, made in 1924, that "a faith on the defensive is confessedly senile."[6] It is true that

[2]Nels F. S. Ferré, *The Christian Fellowship* (New York, 1940), p. 111.

[3]*Cf.* Harrison S. Elliott, *Can Religious Education Be Christian?* (New York, 1940).

[4]"Religious Education Is in Peril," *International Journal of Religious Education*, XXXIII (1939), p. 10. See also "The Assault Upon Liberalism," *Religious Education*, XXXIV (1939), pp. 85-92.

[5]William C. Bower, "The Challenge of Reaction to Liberal Thought," *Religious Education*, XXXII (1937), pp. 117-124; "Points of Tension Between Progressive Religious Education and Current Theological Trends," *ibid.*, XXXIV (1939), pp. 164-172; F. Ernest Johnson, "Religious Education and the Theological Trend," *ibid.*, XXXIII (1938), pp. 82-86; Stewart G. Cole, "Where Religious Education and Theology Meet," *ibid.*, XXXV (1940), pp. 18-25.

[6]*The Faith of Modernism* (New York, 1924), p. 1.

the newer theological views are, in many respects, defective from the standpoint of a constructive theory of Christian nurture. But it seems no less true that traditional religious liberalism is even more fatally defective in its doctrine of Christian nurture. Thus it appears reasonable to contend that the primary obligation of liberal educators is to recognize and seek to correct the weaknesses of their own religious faith. Only thus does it seem possible to reinvigorate the work of Christian nurture.

2. *Historic Tendencies of Liberalism*

THIS BOOK concerns itself with contemporary problems of liberal faith and nurture. The most basic current problems, however, are the outgrowth, directly or indirectly, of tendencies of religious thought which emerged long before the advent of the twentieth century. It is thus in the interest of clarifying current issues to make a brief survey of the historical tendencies that lie back of present-day liberalism.

The liberal movement in American religious thought has a much longer history than is commonly supposed. It takes in not merely the nineteenth century, but most of the eighteenth.[1] The Age of Reason exercised a much wider influence in eighteenth-century America than most people realize; and it gave rise to tendencies of thought that have characterized certain phases of liberalism ever since.[2]

Twentieth-century liberalism, however, is more vitally

[1] Taken in its broadest meaning, religious liberalism even antedates the eighteenth century. See Charles Lyttle, "A Sketch of the Theological Development of Harvard University, 1636–1805," *Church History,* v (1936), pp. 301–321.

[2] For recent accounts of eighteenth-century liberalism, see G. A. Koch, *Republican Religion* (New York, 1933); H. M. Morais, *Deism in Eighteenth Century America* (New York, 1934); N. H. Sonne, *Liberal Kentucky* (New York, 1939).

connected with that type of liberal theology which became articulate in the thought of three New England clergymen— William E. Channing, Theodore Parker, and Horace Bushnell. All three were nurtured in the faith of what is called the New England Theology, an Edwardian version of Calvinism. They were all originally members of the Congregational Church, but in the end only Bushnell remained a member of that body. Channing and Parker, who in many respects were more radical than Bushnell, became influential leaders in the Unitarian fellowship. Of the three, only Bushnell became directly identified with the modern theory of Christian nurture. Yet from the standpoint of the theological framework of that theory, the views of both Channing and Parker must be regarded as an integral part of it.

No attempt will be made here to give either a comprehensive or a detailed account of the development of theological liberalism in the nineteenth century.[3] We shall merely sketch in brief outline four major tendencies which emerged during the latter half of that century and which moulded decisively the underlying theological thought of Christian nurture in the twentieth century. To be sure, these are by no means the only tendencies that may be found in nineteenth-century liberalism; nevertheless, they do seem to be the more influential ones.

(a) *Divine immanence*. The emergence of liberalism in America is closely related to the decline and collapse of New England Calvinism of the Edwardian type. Central in that

[3]Valuable surveys of the growth of liberalism during the last half of the nineteenth century may be found in J. W. Buckham, *Progressive Religious Thought in America* (Boston, 1919); F. H. Foster, *The Modern Movement in American Theology* (New York, 1939); and C. H. Hopkins, *The Rise of the Social Gospel in American Protestantism, 1865–1915* (New Haven, 1940).

system of thought was the idea of a transcendent God. In the period of its supremacy it had tended, at times, so to magnify God's sovereignty as to deny, or at least to obscure, the fact of His indwelling presence. The idea of God as distant had usually overshadowed the idea of God as near and intimate. The idea of God as spectacularly and intermittently active in the world had all but obscured the idea of God as continuously operative within the world process. The principle of discontinuity was clearly the major principle of New England orthodoxy.

Liberal theology from the first revolted against this mode of thought. Whereas orthodoxy construed the world process in terms of two sharply dissociated orders of events—the natural and the supernatural—liberalism sought to conceive the world process in terms of a unified and dynamic order of events. Whereas orthodoxy made the principle of discontinuity primary, liberalism made the principle of continuity primary.[4] Thus at the outset liberalism necessarily tended in the direction of some form of divine immanence.

This trend is reflected in the religious thought of Horace Bushnell, whom Walter M. Horton recently called "the Schleiermacher of American liberalism."[5] Basic in Bushnell's system of religious thought is the idea of God as the indwelling reality of one organic and developing world-process.[6]

[4]That this has been the ruling positive principle throughout the history of American liberalism has been pointed out by several writers, including John C. Bennett, "After Liberalism—What?" *Christian Century,* L (1933), pp. 1403–1406; Walter M. Horton, *Realistic Theology,* p. 33; H. P. Van Dusen, "The Liberal Movement in Theology," in *The Church Through Half a Century,* ed. S. M. Cavert and H. P. Van Dusen (New York, 1936), p. 77.

[5]*Realistic Theology,* p. 27.

[6]This fact is made quite explicit in Bushnell's later writings, for example, "Science and Religion," *Putnam's Magazine,* I (1868), pp. 265–275.

This idea is implicit in his doctrine of Christian nurture. It is only on the belief that God is immanent in the world of man that the child could be expected to grow up within the Kingdom of God through participation in the organic life of the Christian family. In his *Nature and the Supernatural*,[7] Bushnell sought to modify the rigidities of supernaturalism in such fashion as to afford the basis for a concept of divine immanence. He seems to have sensed the fact that unless the old barriers between the natural and the supernatural could be broken down and "one system of God" be established, the principle of immanence as presupposed in his theory of Christian nurture would rest upon an insecure foundation. On the other hand, he became increasingly fearful lest the rising tide of naturalistic thought should undermine Christian faith.[8] If traditional supernaturalism was no longer convincing to him, he yet drew back from the implications of naturalism. Thus Bushnell undertook to maintain the principle of "the rigid unity of the system of God," and yet make a real place for the activity of the supernatural in that unified system.[9] How successful he was in his efforts seems debatable. Nevertheless, he opened a way to mitigate some of the cruder forms of supernaturalism.

It remained for Theodore Parker to champion a more extreme type of religious immanentism and to make a more complete break with supernatural theology. He embraced with enthusiasm the more radical religious ideas of France and Germany, and he lamented the fact that "there is no

[7]New York, 1858.

[8]This fear is clearly reflected in the second edition of *Nature and the Supernatural* (New York, 1864), pp. 20-31.

[9]*Ibid.*, p. 31.

science of theology with us."[10] In place of the speculative and dogmatic theological method of orthodoxy, he advocated the method of empirical science. "A real theology," he says, "must be made up from facts with consciousness and observation, and like all science is capable of demonstration."[11]

Parker's so-called "scientific theology" led him to a wholesale rejection of the "monstrous doctrines" of supernaturalism.[12] He was impatient with any doctrine of divine action that represented God as miraculously invading the orderly processes of the natural world. For him, God is perpetually and universally immanent in the world of nature and of man. "The powers of matter," he contends, "are but modes of God's activity; nature lives in him—without his continual active presence therein nature were not. . . . He is equally present in the world of man, the world of spirit; it also depends upon him; he lives in it, and it in him."[13] Although Parker professed to believe in divine transcendence, his extreme emphasis upon divine immanence led his own contemporaries to accuse him of being a pantheist.[14]

In America the great age of theological emphasis upon immanence centers in the period between the Civil War and the first World War. A major factor in this emphasis was the growth of modern evolutionary science. In the early 1880's Theodore T. Munger, an ardent disciple of Bushnell, frequently urged that Christian thinkers recognize the posi-

[10]*The Transient and Permanent in Christianity* (Cent. ed., Boston, 1908), ed. G. W. Cooke, p. 159.

[11]*Ibid.,* p. 305.   [12]*Ibid.,* pp. 303–304.

[13]*Ibid.,* p. 313. See also Parker's *A Discourse of Matters Pertaining to Religion,* ed. T. W. Higginson (Cent. ed., Boston, 1907), pp. 151–161.

[14]John W. Chadwick, *Theodore Parker, Preacher and Reformer* (Boston, 1901), p. 194.

tive values in the theory of evolution. For him, evolution was "not something to be quelled, but an ally to be pressed into service."[15] He saw evolutionary science serving Christian faith in a threefold fashion: (1) As introducing the principle of unity into the universe; (2) as laying the basis for a developmental conception of religion; and (3) as "drawing God down and into the processes of creation as a constant and all-pervasive factor."[16]

The impetus given to the doctrine of divine immanence by the idea of evolution is evident in the writings of such popular religious leaders as John Fiske,[17] Henry Ward Beecher,[18] and Lyman Abbott.[19] The latter voiced the sentiment of all three when he pointed out that the Church "is coming more and more to conceive of God, not as some one outside of his creation ruling *over* it, but as some one inside his creation ruling *within* it."[20] Liberal theologians of this period, no less than liberal clergymen, found convincing support for divine immanence in the doctrine of evolution, even though they usually exercised more critical caution in stating the nature and limits of evolution.[21]

On the basis of this brief sketch, it can be seen that the idea of an immanent God became increasingly ·popular as the nineteenth century approached its end. In 1895, Washington Gladden pointed out that the concept of divine im-

[15]*The Freedom of Faith* (Boston, 1883), p. 67.

[16]*The Appeal to Life* (Boston, 1887), p. 219.

[17]*Outlines of Cosmic Philosophy* (Boston, 1874); *Through Nature to God* (Boston, 1899); *The Idea of God* (Boston, 1892).

[18]*Evolution and Religion* (Boston, 1885).

[19]*The Evolution of Christianity* (Boston, 1892); *The Theology of an Evolutionist* (Boston, 1898).

[20]*The Evolution of Christianity,* pp. 109–110.

[21]*Cf.* Henry Churchill King, *Reconstruction in Theology* (New York, 1901), Chap. VII.

manence had already become one of the ruling theological ideas.[22] Gladden's own thought, and especially his theology of the social gospel, is rooted in the doctrine of God's immanence in the world of man and of nature.[23] It is thus not surprising that this idea should have become the most absorbing theme of theologians in the early part of the twentieth century.[24]

(*b*) *Growth.* A second major concept in the development of liberal Protestantism is the idea of growth. This idea has had a threefold application in the rise of religious liberalism: (1) growth of religion in the individual; (2) growth of religion in the race; and (3) growth as a mode of achieving individual and social change.

Central in Bushnell's doctrine of religious nurture is the idea that the child is to be a growing Christian.[25] The concept of moral and religious growth in the race seems to have been equally basic with him.[26] In his view of moral progress, he was able to say that slavery was relatively a good thing in the age of the Bible and yet an evil in the nineteenth century.[27] He was certain, at least in his earlier life, that human history "must ultimately issue in a moral age."[28] While he said, "I anticipate no perfect state," yet he argued that "a day will come when the dominion of ignorance and physical force, when distinctions of blood and the accidents of fortune

[22]*The Ruling Ideas of the Present Age* (New York, 1895), p. 294.
[23]*Ibid.,* Chap. xi. See also *How Much Is Left of the Old Doctrines?* (New York, 1899), Chaps. ii-iii.
[24]Francis J. McConnell, *The Diviner Immanence* (New York, 1906), p. 6. See also Henry Churchill King, *Theology and the Social Consciousness* (New York, 1902), pp. 40–42.
[25]*Christian Nurture* (Cent. ed., New York, 1910), p. 10.
[26]*Work and Play* (Cent. ed., New York, 1910), pp. 78–123.
[27]*Ibid.,* p. 94.   [28]*Ibid.,* p. 117.

will cease to rule the world."[29] War will be abolished, he said, "by the progress of liberty and intelligence."[30]

The idea of progress in terms of gradual growth was cardinal with Bushnell. Revolutionary and catastrophic change was alien to his mode of life and thought. One of his main objections to the religious revivalism of his day was that it undertook to bring in the Kingdom of God by sudden conquest. He was definitely opposed to those social and religious radicals of his day who countenanced revolutionary tactics in the abolition of slavery. In his view, slavery would be abolished gradually by a process of moral evolution, and without any resort to methods of social violence.

In Theodore Parker the idea of a continuously growing religion in the life of the race had a militant apostle. Coming under the early influence of German historical and biblical criticism, he said: "All the writings in the New Testament, as well as the Old, contain marks of their human origin, of human weakness and imperfection."[31] Assuming that revelation is progressive, he urged that it "is only impious superstition that dares foreshorten God, and say that there is for man no higher revelation than past times can bring."[32]

Parker's idea of a continuously developing religion was much too radical for even the more advanced liberals of his generation. But the emergence of the Darwinian theory of evolution was shortly to bring about a revolutionary.shift in American theology. Contrary to a general opinion, the idea of evolution took root rather quickly in American theology. Darwin's *Origin of Species,* first published in England in

[29]*Ibid.,* p. 118.   [30]*Ibid.,* p. 119.
[31]*A Discourse of Matters Pertaining to Religion,* p. 320.
[32]*The Transient and Permanent in Christianity,* p. 67.

1859, was brought out in an American edition in 1860.[33] A vigorous debate took place at once, especially in respect to its religious implications.[34] Controversy raged for many years to come. In the earlier stages of the discussion evolution, as a rule, met with marked disfavor in religious circles.[35] Yet in a comparatively short time evolutionary modes of thought met with growing sympathy among a few of the bolder thinkers.[36] The seventies witnessed in certain circles an aggressive defense of evolution. For example, a rising young clergyman, Newman Smyth, challenged the scientifically timid churchmen of his day with the statement: "Whoever is afraid of science does not believe in God!"[37] "We admit," he says, "that the course of visible nature can be best summed up in some general law of evolution."[38] A few years later Theodore T. Munger spoke in equally challenging terms. "The timid may linger on the threshold," he said, "but the time has come to enter in and set the Faith face to face with this principle (evolution) that now colors and dominates all thought."[39] With the advent of the nineties Lyman Abbott wrote: "Christianity is an evolution, a growing revelation of God . . . a revelation which is itself the secret and the power

[33]Appleton: New York.

[34]See Sidney Ratner, "Evolution and the Rise of the Scientific Spirit in America," *Philosophy of Science*, III (1936), pp. 105–122.

[35]Even Bushnell rejected the Darwinian theory of the transmutation of species, and concluded that if it should be proven true, "we may well enough agree to live without religion." "Science and Religion," *Putnam's Magazine*, I (1868), p. 271.

[36]Ratner, *op. cit.*, pp. 108, 110–114.

[37]*Old Faiths in New Light* (New York, 1879), p. 24. *Cf.* James Freeman Clarke, *Steps of Belief* (Boston, 1870); James McCosh, *Christianity and Positivism* (New York, 1871).

[38]Smyth, *op. cit.*, p. 383.

[39]*The Freedom of Faith*, p. 67. See also his essay "Evolution and the Faith" in *The Appeal to Life*, pp. 209–243.

of a growing spiritual life in man, beginning in the early dawn of human history . . . and to be consummated no one can tell when or how."[40] Thus it is clear that evolution had a decisive influence on all three aspects of American religious thought. Ideas such as Bushnell had expressed in an earlier generation were now provided with new and more secure foundations.

The closing decades of the nineteenth century witnessed a far-flung movement in the field of genetic psychology. No person was a greater factor in this movement than the ardent evolutionist, G. Stanley Hall. In 1882, Hall published an article on the religious nurture of children in which he advanced ideas that were destined to be a major factor in shaping the educational theory of the Protestant churches up through at least the first decade of the twentieth century. In this he set forth his famous view that the child in his mental, moral, and religious growth rehearses or recapitulates the stages of development through which the race has already passed.[41] On this hypothesis, he advanced the idea that the church school curriculum for a particular age-group should be composed of the moral and religious concepts and ideals of the culture-epoch through which the child of that age was passing. Thus he argued that the Old Testament, rather than the New, should be used in the religious nurture of childhood.[42]

Hall's doctrine of recapitulation is today generally discredited, but it exercised considerable influence on the theory

[40]*The Evolution of Christianity,* pp. 255–256.
[41]"The Moral and Religious Training of Children," *The Princeton Review,* 4th ser., LVIII (1882), p. 32. For a more detailed account of the theory of recapitulation, see his *Adolescence,* Vol. I (New York, 1904), pp. 2–3; 44–50; 55–57.
[42]"The Moral and Religious Training of Children," *op. cit.,* p. 42.

of religious education in the period prior to the first World War. The lingering tendency in certain circles to break up the period of childhood into "stages," and to segregate children into sharply defined age-groups, derives largely from the genetic child-study movement that was popularized by Hall.

The doctrine of evolution gave important support to the idea of gradual change in the religious life of the individual and of society. Wherever intellectual and religious liberals adopted evolutionary modes of thought, they generally became ardent exponents of the idea of gradual, rather than of revolutionary, change. In the thought of Hall, for example, the concept of change in terms of evolutionary growth is basic. In the article already referred to, he contends that as mankind "becomes truly civilized revolutions cease to be sudden and violent, and become gradually transitory and without abrupt change."[43] Religion in the individual, he says, also should be a gradually developing experience. Hall sharply criticizes those churchmen who look upon "change of heart as an instantaneous conquest rather than as growth."[44]

From this account, it should surprise no one that the idea of growth became one of the most conspicuous emphases in the rise of twentieth-century education, whether secular or religious. It was this idea, perhaps as no other, that brought modern education and liberal Christianity into fruitful co-operation.[45]

(c) *The goodness of man.* No idea of orthodox faith was more offensive to nineteenth-century liberals than the notion

[43]*Ibid.*, p. 48.   [44]*Loc. cit.*
[45]*See,* for example, John Dewey's significant address, "Religious Education as Conditioned by Modern Psychology and Pedagogy" in *Proceedings of the First Annual Convention of the Religious Education Association,* 1903, pp. 60–66.

of human depravity. Early in the century, they, in contrast to orthodox churchmen, became vigorous advocates of a sunny view of man. Thus Henry Ware of Harvard wrote: "I insist, that if we take a fair and full view, we shall find that wickedness, far from being the prevailing part of the human character, makes but an inconsiderable part of it. That in by far the largest part of human beings, the just, and kind, and benevolent dispositions prevail beyond measure over the opposite; and that even in the worst men good feelings and principles are predominant, and they probably perform in the course of their lives many more good than bad actions."[46] Moreover, whatever wickedness one does find in the world, is, says Ware, the fruit of a wrong education and of an anti-social environment.[47]

The basic element of Channing's theology is the doctrine of man's inherent divinity. Nowhere is this idea set forth more clearly than in his famous discourse, "Likeness to God," preached at an ordination service in 1828. "In Christianity," he says, "I meet perpetual testimonies to the divinity of human nature."[48] Since man has within his nature the seeds of divinity, he may grow godlike by the gradual unfolding of his own inner nature. Furthermore, this unfolding process need not produce in man any experience of inner conflict. All such conflict does violence to human nature. "Our proper work," he says, "is to approach God by the free and natural unfolding of our highest powers—of understanding, conscience, love and the moral will."[49]

[46]*Letters Addressed to Trinitarians and Calvinists* (Cambridge, 1820), p. 18.
[47]*Ibid.*, p. 19.
[48]*The Works of William E. Channing,* D.D. (New ed., Boston, 1882), p. 292.
[49]*Ibid.*, p. 297.

The idea of human goodness made an equally strong appeal to Parker. He professes surprise that any person "can think meanly of this chief creation of God" when one considers what "a panorama of triumph lies there behind us."[50] If only the teacher of religion saw man in proper historical perspective, he could ."demonstrate the nobility of our nature, and show the certainty of our triumph at the last over all the transient evils of our condition."[51] Religion should not seek to regenerate man, to change human nature, but only to develop nature from within.[52]

Bushnell was less romantic than Parker in his analysis of human nature. "The perfectibility of man," he admits, "is forever excluded here by the tenor of his existence."[53] Nevertheless, the discourse in which that admission occurs is rooted in the assumption that man's continuous moral progress is certain. While man will always "make experiment of evil," he will at the same time know that the law of love in man will triumph. On this basis Bushnell viewed the future optimistically, and he urged the Yale alumni to whom he spoke to "have faith in the future." Persons of the backward look he likened to "owls flying toward the dawn and screaming."[54] Waxing eloquent over the greatness of American institutions, he assured his youthful hearers that "everything true, just, pure, good, great, can here unfold itself without obstruction."[55]

As one might suppose, the idea of man's growing goodness was given great impetus through the spread of the

---

[50]*The Transient and Permanent in Christianity,* pp. 307–308.
[51]*Ibid.,* p. 308.   [53]*Work and Play,* p. 118.
[52]*Ibid.,* p. 359.   [54]*Ibid.,* p. 122.
[55]*Ibid.,* p. 123. Bushnell's later writings, however, reflect much less optimism concerning human nature and social history. *See,* for example, *Nature and the Supernatural,* new ed., Chaps. IV–VIII.

popular concepts of Darwinian evolution. This is demonstrated, for example, in the popular lectures and writings of John Fiske, who was an enthusiastic Darwinian. In an address to the Concord School of Philosophy in 1884, Fiske said, "Man is slowly passing from a primitive social state in which he was little better than a brute, toward an ultimate social state in which his character shall become so transformed that nothing of the brute can be detected in it. The ape and the tiger in human nature will become extinct. . . . The modern prophet, employing the method of science, may again proclaim that the kingdom of heaven is at hand."[56]

This general point of view became increasingly popular among religious liberals in the closing years of the nineteenth century. Not all of them, of course, spoke in the romantic terms of a Fiske. On the whole, however, they were optimistic in their interpretations of human nature.[57]

(d) *The historical Jesus.* A fourth characteristic aspect of religious liberalism in the nineteenth century was its emphasis upon the historical Jesus. One result of this emphasis was the writing of numerous books on the life of Jesus. In 1901, Henry Churchill King wrote: "It is a most significant fact that every single great life of Christ since the Gospels is the product of the last sixty-five years."[58]

This life-of-Jesus emphasis in modern theology was a

[56]*Studies in Religion,* Vol. ix: *Miscellaneous Writings of John Fiske* (Boston, 1902), p. 72. Fiske's *Outlines of Cosmic Philosophy,* first published in 1874, provides a general framework for this optimistic theory of man.

[57]*See,* for example, the views of so cautious a liberal as George A. Gordon, *The New Epoch for Faith* (Boston, 1901), pp. 18; 79–83; 387–389; *Ultimate Conceptions of Faith* (Boston, 1903), pp. 237–243; 246–249.

[58]*Reconstruction in Theology,* p. 186.

unique product of Protestant liberalism.[59] That it reflects a reorientation in christological thought hardly can be denied.[60] The initial premise with which Protestant liberals have sought to apprehend the nature of Jesus is strikingly different from that of earlier Christian thinkers. Harry Emerson Fosdick has stated this contrast succinctly: "They started with the certainty that Jesus came from the divine realm and then wondered how he could be truly man; we start from the certainty that he was genuinely man and then wonder in what sense he can be God."[61]

The modern quest for the historic Jesus began in the period of the Enlightenment, but its full vigor was not felt in America until the latter part of the nineteenth century.[62] In this search, the method used was historical criticism applied to the writings of the New Testament. This method assumed that an objective analysis of the Gospels as historical documents would disclose "the man Jesus" which lay be-

[59]It was in 1835 that the Hegelian David F. Strauss published his epoch-making *Leben Jesu*, and produced thereby a near-panic in the theological world because of its sweeping rejection of older christological views. *Cf.* O. Pfleiderer, *The Development of Theology in Germany Since Kant* (London, 1909), pp. 132–133; H. R. Macintosh, *Types of Modern Theology* (London, 1939), pp. 118–121; Shirley Jackson Case, "The Ethics of Jesus from Strauss to Barth," *Journal of Religion,* xv (1935), pp. 389–399.

[60]*Cf.* A. C. McGiffert, *Christianity as History and Faith,* ed. A. C. McGiffert, Jr. (New York, 1934), pp. 107–113.

[61]*The Modern Use of the Bible* (New York, 1924), p. 256. *See also* McGiffert, *op. cit.,* p. 107.

[62]Valuable surveys of this development may be found in Albert Schweitzer, *The Quest of the Historical Jesus* (Eng. tr., London, 1910); Friedrich Loofs, *What is the Truth about Jesus Christ?* (Edinburgh, 1913); Heinrich Weinel and Alban G. Widgery, *Jesus in the Nineteenth Century and After* (Edinburgh, 1914); Shirley Jackson Case, *Jesus Through the Centuries* (Chicago, 1932), pp. 289–345; C. C. McCown, *The Search for the Real Jesus* (New York, 1940).

neath the christological colorings of the early Church.[63] The advent of the present century found liberal scholars in America, as elsewhere, believing that they had really discovered the historic Jesus. "The greatest fact in modern Christian history," said McGiffert in 1909, "is the rediscovery of Jesus."[64] What, then, is the character of this new Jesus? He is one who "speaks a language which the modern age, with its genial confidence in man, its vivid interest in the present world and its profound concern for social betterment, is peculiarly fitted to understand."[65] In other words, the real Jesus is a twentieth-century modernist!

Aside from the question of whether this is a true understanding of Jesus, it represents an emphasis that had been gathering force for a long time. Evidences of this tendency may be found in American culture as early as the middle of the eighteenth century.[66] Inspired though it was by German, English, and French antecedents, it had a ready, although sporadic, response among native Americans. While it made little headway among the clergy, it met with favor among such influential laymen as Thomas Jefferson. "I am a Christian," wrote Jefferson, "in the only sense he [Jesus] wished any one to be; sincerely attached to his doctrines, in preference to all others; ascribing to himself every human excellence; and believing he never claimed any other."[67]

This general idea of Jesus comes out clearly in Channing's

[63]C. H. Dodd, *History and the Gospel* (New York, 1938), p. 11.
[64]*Christianity as History and Faith*, p. 302.
[65]*Ibid.*, p. 303.
[66]*See* Frank H. Foster, *A Genetic History of the New England Theology* (Chicago, 1907), pp. 273–281; Morais, *Deism in Eighteenth Century America;* Koch, *Republican Religion.*
[67]*The Writings of Thomas Jefferson,* ed. Paul Lester Ford (New York, 1892), Vol. VIII, p. 223. *Cf.* B. T. Schantz, "Ethan Allen's Religious Ideas," *The Journal of Religion,* XVIII (1938), pp. 183–217.

famous discourse, "Unitarian Christianity," preached at Baltimore in 1819. This sermon provoked a barrage of open letters, pro and con.[68] The fires of conflict raged for many
years, leaving behind them embers of hate and division that
were to flare up again and again during the remainder of
the century.

It is not necessary here to dwell on Channing's concept
of Jesus. It is well known that he, like Jefferson, repudiated
orthodox trinitarianism.[69] In regard to the person of Jesus,
he said, "We believe that Jesus is one mind, one soul, one
being, as truly one as we are, and equally distinct from the
one God. We complain of the doctrine of the Trinity, that,
not satisfied with making God three beings, it makes Jesus
Christ two beings, and thus introduces infinite confusion into
our conceptions of his character."[70] In a beautiful sermon
on "The Imitableness of Christ's Character," he said: "The
mind of Jesus Christ, my hearer, and your mind are of one
family; nor was there any thing in his of which you have
not the principle, the capacity, the promise in yourself."[71]

[68]Among the more influential writers were Moses Stuart, *Letters
to the Rev. William E. Channing Containing Remarks on His Sermon Recently Preached and Published at Baltimore* (Andover, 1819);
Leonard Woods, *Letters to Unitarians, Occasioned by the Sermon of
Rev. Wm. E. Channing at the Ordination of the Rev. J. Sparks*
(Andover, 1820); Henry Ware, *Letters Addressed to Trinitarians and
Calvinists, Occasioned by Dr. Woods' Letters to Unitarians* (Cambridge, 1820). The first edition of Stuart's letters was exhausted in a
week, and of the other editions which rapidly followed, "four or five
were soon printed in England, with the highest commendation." Ed-
wards A. Park, *Discourse Delivered at the Funeral of Professor Moses
Stuart* (Boston, 1852), p. 29.

[69]*Works of William E. Channing,* pp. 371–376.

[70]*Ibid.,* p. 373. *See also* pp. 243–244; 387–388; 402.

[71]*Ibid.,* p. 313. In this same discourse, however, he seemingly contradicts himself by the assertion, "I believe him [Jesus] to be a more
than human being." P. 312.

Channing believed that if the historical Jesus were freed from the entanglements of a false and superstitious theology, modern man would readily accept his teachings.

In Theodore Parker one meets an even more vigorous plea for a recovery of the historical Jesus. The earliest gospel records, he argued, presented Jesus as only a man. Later interpreters, notably Paul, introduced the idea of a metaphysical Jesus.[72] Of Jesus he wrote: "I think him human, not superhuman, the manliest of men."[73] With Jefferson and Channing, Parker contended that the major obstacle to the spread of Christianity lay in its false Christology. Jesus, he said, makes his greatest appeal when he is presented as "a man of genius."[74]

With Horace Bushnell there emerged in American religious thought a type of liberal Christology that failed to fit exclusively into the ideology either of current orthodoxy or of Unitarianism. Bushnell believed himself to be orthodox; yet current orthodoxy sharply criticized his idea of Jesus. On the other hand, Unitarians did not find his view of Jesus satisfactory to them. The fact seems to be that he recognized elements of truth in both parties, yet not enough in either, or in both, to do justice to his understanding of Jesus.

Bushnell claimed to stand firmly with orthodoxy in maintaining the divinity of Jesus Christ. Christ "differs from us, not in degree, but in kind."[75] On the other hand, he criticized orthodoxy's tendency toward tritheism as vigorously as Channing. "No soul," he said, "can truly rest in God,

[72]The Transient and Permanent in Christianity, p. 275.
[73]Ibid., p. 465.
[74]Discourse of Matters Pertaining to Religion, p. 275.
[75]God in Christ (Cent. ed., New York, 1910), p. 123. See also his Nature and the Supernatural (new ed., New York, 1868), Chap. x.

when God is two or three."[76] To be sure, he advocated the idea of an "instrumental trinity"; yet he argued that this idea did not in any way contradict the principle of the essential unity of God.[77] Furthermore, Bushnell could find "no solid foundation for the common trinitarian theory of two distinct or distinctly active subsistences in the person of Christ."[78] One of Bushnell's main objections to the current two-nature theory of Jesus' person was that it denied in effect a real incarnation. If the divine side of Christ did not really unite with the human so as to constitute one being, then God did not really become manifest in the flesh. "Meanwhile the whole work of Christ, as a subject, suffering Redeemer, is thrown upon the human side of his nature, and the divine side standing thus aloof, incommunicably distant, has nothing to do with the transaction, other than to be a spectator of it."[79] He therefore held immovably to the unity of Christ's person. He also believed in the Incarnation. Jesus "is in and of the race, born of a woman, living in the line of humanity, subject to human conditions, an integral part, in one view, of the world's history; only bringing into it, and setting in organic union with it, the Eternal Life."[80]

In respect of Christ's redemptive work, Bushnell was as convinced as Channing that the penal theory of the atonement was untenable.[81] For him it had two basic defects. First, it denied the ethical character of God as love. Second, it failed to take account of the fact that the vicarious sacrifice of Christ is in principle at the heart of all true love, and therefore reproducible in the moral experience of all re-

[76]*God in Christ*, p. 134.
[77]*Ibid.*, pp. 174–177.   [79]*Loc. cit.*
[78]*Ibid.*, p. 155.   [80]*Ibid.*, p. 165.
[81]*Ibid.*, pp. 192–202. *See also* his *The Vicarious Sacrifice* (2nd ed., New York, 1866), pp. 41; 45–46; 71–72.

deemed men. It was the second defect that gave Bushnell most concern. He argued vigorously against those who limited vicarious sacrifice to Jesus.[82] This is the root, according to him, of the "amazing dullness of the gospel."[83] In their zeal to exalt Christ, orthodox Christians had unwittingly destroyed the point of contact between themselves and Christ. Orthodoxy admonishes men to take up the cross and follow Christ, yet men "are to bear the cross for the discipline, and not for what love sees to be won by a cross. Thus the orthodox idea of the cross becomes a dry, stunted, half conception of it."[84]

Bushnell proposes a more dynamic conception of vicarious sacrifice. He takes the position that love is itself an essentially vicarious principle. In his vivid phrase, "There is a Gethsemane hid in all love."[85] "Such is love that it must insert itself into the conditions, burden itself with the wants, and woes, and losses, and even wrongs of others."[86] Thus Christ in his vicarious sacrifice "simply fulfils what belongs universally to love; doing neither more nor less than what the common standard of holiness and right requires."[87] Following out courageously the logic of this process of reasoning, Bushnell concludes that the vicarious suffering of Jesus was "in no way peculiar to him, save in degree." Sacrifice in man is therefore not different from sacrifice in Christ, save that in man it "carries humbler effects."[88]

This element of Bushnell's thought is perhaps his most original contribution to the doctrine of Christian redemption. It has had a profound influence on the subsequent de-

[82]*The Vicarious Sacrifice*, pp. 105–118.
[83]*Ibid.*, pp. 124–125.
[84]*Ibid.*, p. 126.
[85]*Ibid.*, p. 47.
[86]*Ibid.*, p. 107.
[87]*Ibid.*, p. 105.
[88]*Ibid.*, p. 107.

velopment of liberal views of the relation of Jesus Christ to men in the work of redemption. Its major implications, therefore, should be made clear in this connection. Basic in Bushnell's idea of the atonement is the assumption that every redeemed person belongs to the very process by which Christ himself became Redeemer. His ablest biographer, Theodore T. Munger, expressed the view that Bushnell taught "that Christ does nothing for a man beyond what the man himself is required to do for other men."[89] There may be some doubt as to whether Bushnell went quite as far as Munger claims. Yet this idea is strongly suggested in some of his writing. According to Bushnell, "We, as a race, in being restored to God, are to be perfected in the common universal standard of goodness, and so to be established with Christ in the same way of sacrifice."[90] He reminds men that they should not set themselves up as "redeemers"; yet the only reason that they should not do so is because "our petty measures of quantity and character forbid such a thought."[91]

Bushnell's emphasis at this point served as a corrective of that mode of orthodox thought that had set vicarious sacrifice wholly beyond the plane of human experience. His idea that truly "Christed" persons really share in the atoning work of God contains an element of truth that is essential to vital Christian discipleship. In an important sense the Christian is required to take up the cross and follow Christ.[92] Yet in his tendency to equate the cross of Christ with that of Christ's followers Bushnell set a definite trend toward an attenuated Christology.

[89]*Horace Bushnell, Preacher and Theologian* (Boston, 1899), p. 269.
[90]*The Vicarious Sacrifice,* p. 113. *See also* pp. 114–123.
[91]*Ibid.,* p. 124.
[92]On this point, *see* James Moffatt's illuminating comment in *Jesus Christ the Same* (New York, 1940), pp. 99–111.

The closing years of the nineteenth century reveal a marked trend in liberal circles toward a reduced Christology. America's greatest theologian in the Bushnellian tradition, George A. Gordon, bore striking testimony to this fact. "In the minds of the younger men," he wrote in 1890, "one finds metaphysical infirmity and agnosticism joined with the sincerest homage in the presence of Jesus. The purely ethical apprehension of Christ is coming to be the fashion."[93] According to Gordon, "otherness in Christ to humanity" counts for nothing with many leading liberals.[94] "If there is complete identity between Christ and humanity in respect of being and range of powers, men are ready to believe on him; but if it is said that there is any otherness, any eternal difference between him and his brethren, it is felt that that must be a metaphysical fiction. Christ gives the possible stature of every man, and that we readily accept; he reveals the point at which every human life touches the Eternal Fatherhood, and that we willingly believe. But that Jesus should sustain to God a relation singular, inapproachable, ineffable, is today either denied outright or admitted blindly."[95]

This trend to equate the person and work of Jesus with that of other men Gordon vigorously resisted.[96] Nothing could so weaken the force of the gospel, he thought, as a deficient Christology.[97] This general drift was to continue, despite the protests of men like Gordon. Toward the close of the century the Christological interpretations of Schleiermacher and Ritschl became increasingly influential in the

[93]*The Christ of Today* (6th ed., Boston, 1895), p. 54.
[94]*Ibid.*, p. 94.   [95]*Ibid.*, p. 96.
[96]*Ibid.*, pp. 93–136. *See also* "The Collapse of the New England Theology," *The Harvard Theological Review*, I (1908), pp. 165–167.
[97]*Ultimate Conceptions of Faith* (Boston, 1903), p. 291.

thinking of American religious liberals.[98] Theology became more and more Christocentric in its emphasis; nevertheless, Christ himself became for a growing number of liberals little more than the ethical prophet of Nazareth. New Testament research gave support to this general trend in Christology.[99] "At the close of last century," says E. F. Scott, "New Testament Scholars, in spite of their numberless differences on points of detail, were agreed on the general interpretation of the life and work of Jesus. He was the prophet of a new righteousness, based on a new conception of the nature of God and of man's relation to God."[100]

3. The Emergence of Liberalism in Contemporary Religious Education

THE EFFORT to set theological liberalism in its historical perspective becomes relevant to our main problem when we recognize the fact that just here lie the roots of the assumptions and guiding notions which became the stock-in-trade for the theories of the religious educators of the twentieth century. Reflecting on a quarter-century of religious education in America, Gerald Birney Smith, in 1928, wrote: "Perhaps nowhere else [than in religious education] can we see more clearly the direction in which religious thinking is moving."[1] The truth of this statement can hardly be denied

[98] A brief account of these and other influences from abroad is given in Frank H. Foster, *The Modern Movement in American Theology* (New York, 1939), Chap. VII.

[99] *See* Shirley Jackson Case, "The Ethics of Jesus from Strauss to Barth," *Journal of Religion,* xv (1935), pp. 393–394.

[100] "The Significance of Jesus for Modern Religion in View of His Eschatological Teaching," *The American Journal of Theology,* XVIII (1914), p. 225.

[1] "Training Christian Ministers," *Religious Education,* XXIII (1928), p. 68.

by any one who is acquainted with the developments of American religious thought. For at no point did liberalism come to more marked expression than in the twentieth-century movement of religious education. This is demonstrated, for example, in the earlier writings of George A. Coe, who, by common consent, is America's most distinguished living philosopher of religious education. Let us, then, examine briefly two of Coe's earlier books from the point of view of the four historic tendencies outlined in the foregoing section of our discussion.

In his *The Religion of a Mature Mind,* published in 1902, Coe revealed a keen insight into the nature and implications of the popular doctrine of divine immanence. He rightly said: "Theology has begun the twentieth century committed to the doctrine of the immanence of God."[2] In this doctrine he envisaged "a wondrous power of dissolving things."[3] Among other things, it dissolved the distinction between religious experience and other types of experience;[4] between the sacred and the secular;[5] between business and devotion;[6] between the divine and the human;[7] between religious education and secular education.[8] The doctrine of divine immanence thus "brings God and the world together at every point."[9]

This general idea became basic in Coe's doctrine of Christian nurture, and through him it became widely influential in the educational philosophy of liberal Protestantism. To be sure, Coe modified his religious and educational thought

[2](New York), p. 219. *Cf.* F. J. McConnell, *The Diviner Immanence* (New York, 1906), p. 6.
[3]*The Religion of a Mature Mind,* p. 332.
[4]*Ibid.,* p. 219.   [7]*Ibid.,* p. 414.
[5]*Ibid.,* p. 332.   [8]*Ibid.,* pp. 298–304.
[6]*Ibid.,* pp. 333–334.   [9]*Ibid.,* p. 347.

as the century progressed. Furthermore, he concerned himself less in later decades with the theological aspects of religion than with the psychological and the social. Nevertheless, the general principle of divine immanence was never
abandoned. Coe's later writings do not, it is true, make use
of the term immanence, but this must not blind one to the
fact that he retains the general principle under other modes
of exposition.

In Coe the concept of growth also had an early and enthusiastic champion, and he gave it a basic place in his theory
of religious nurture. Long in advance of others, he recognized the revolutionary significance of Bushnell's idea of
religious growth in the child, and he did more than any-
body else during the first decade of the twentieth century
to revive Bushnell's doctrine of Christian nurture.[10] In 1904
Coe wrote: "In a word, the very principles for which we
are now struggling to secure recognition were discovered by
Bushnell and applied to our problems as early as 1847."[11]

To Bushnell's concept of growth, however, Coe at once
brought important new support based on the theory of biological and cultural evolution. It was within the framework
of evolutionary science that he thus wrote: "The universe
at large appears to contain a secret spring that pushes life
upward and ever upward."[12] Implicit in this point of view
is the idea of a continuously changing faith, both in the life
of the race and in the life of the individual. The ultimate
implication for religious education was made clear a quarter-century later by Theodore G. Soares, when he said: "We
are making religion anew, as the prophets made it, and as

[10]*Ibid.*, pp. 312–315.
[11]*Education in Religion and Morals* (New York, 1904), p. 384.
[12]*The Religion of a Mature Mind*, p. 396.

Jesus made it."[13] In this view, the value of the Bible lies chiefly in its power to stimulate a religious quest that will result in the creation of spiritual norms that transcend those embodied in the Bible.

The idea of growth as related to the process of individual and social change became influential in Coe's thought. The idea of sudden change, of revolutionary reversal of life-currents, he made secondary to the idea of continuous and gradual growth. The "normal" process of change involves "a community of finite souls progressively realizing their union with one another and with the eternal life of God."[14] Change in the individual is better conceived not as catastrophic and sudden, but as "a normal outcome of wise and continuous training."[15]

Long before the advent of the present century, as we have seen, the idea of the goodness of man had become an integral part of liberal theological thought. Yet in no previous period was that idea proclaimed with such widespread confidence and enthusiasm as in the opening decades of the twentieth century. That Coe had a large part in this general drift of thought can hardly be denied. From the first, he sharply dissented from traditional theologies of sin and evil.[16] The doctrine of depravity, considered in either its milder or its more extreme forms, he regarded as pernicious.[17] It is true that sinful tendencies in human nature were not denied; yet this side of the child's life was certainly not given any prominence. Under the influence of the doc-

[13]*Religious Education* (Chicago, 1928), p. 63.
[14]*The Religion of a Mature Mind*, p. 186.
[15]*Education in Religion and Morals*, p. 394.
[16]*The Religion of a Mature Mind*, Chap. XII.
[17]*Ibid.*, pp. 312–319. See also *Education in Religion and Morals*, pp. 49–60; 65–69.

trine of divine immanence, Coe stressed the fact that within the child-soul there lives the Over Soul.[18] In this view the child is assumed to be in possession of "the life-principle of the kingdom."[19] Children should therefore "be brought to realize that their personality is holy ground."[20] This is the "normal" consciousness of the religiously growing child.[21]

Coe was no less committed to the liberal view of Jesus. In common with other liberals he turned from the Christ of the creeds to Jesus "considered as an historical person."[22] This historic Galilean, the real Jesus, was cast in the role of the supreme Educator.[23] The supremacy of Jesus as educator lay not merely in the fact that his teaching method revealed unexcelled insight into the nature of personality, but also in the fact that he invested human personality with infinite worth and dignity by reason of his true apprehension of the character of God. Above all, this Master-Teacher had a "bright" picture of child-personality, and he taught that "little children" are already in possession of the Kingdom of God.[24]

In light of this analysis of Coe's early thought it is manifest that the contemporary movement of Protestant nurture emerged as an integral part of liberal theological thought. Since the beginning of the twentieth century the theory of religious education has passed through many different phases, as new knowledge has been made available through further research and experimentation. Furthermore, as we shall see, public education in its progressive phase has had

[18]*The Religion of a Mature Mind*, p. 319.
[19]*Education in Religion and Morals*, p. 46.
[20]*Ibid.*, p. 401.
[21]*Ibid.*, p. 47.   [23]*Ibid.*, pp. 405–406.
[22]*Ibid.*, pp. 403–404.   [24]*Ibid.*, pp. 44–45.

a fundamental part in the development of the doctrine of religious nurture. Yet running throughout this entire period of development one can find these same four tendencies of liberal religious thought.

It is thus clear that, historically speaking, the full meaning of religious liberalism cannot be adequately understood merely by conceiving it in terms of a particular method, nor by identifying it with a particular attitude toward truth. To be sure, no one can grasp the full meaning of liberalism unless he comprehends the methodological side of it.[25] Nevertheless, liberalism as a method always involves some sort of creed or definite faith, otherwise it would be meaningless as a religious movement. It is true, of course, that the particular content of liberal faith is subject to change; nevertheless this must not obscure the fact that liberalism at any particular time produces positive affirmations—no matter how tentatively formulated—as well as a method of deriving them. Both aspects of liberalism, therefore, must be considered by any one who desires to understand the full significance of liberal Protestant thought.

From the foregoing historical survey it should be clear that American religious liberalism of the late nineteenth century and the early part of the twentieth reflected a very characteristic *credo*.[26] Though protean in form and constantly changing in content, it yet has been definite enough to be more or less clearly distinguishable from traditional patterns of belief, whether Catholic or Protestant. It is our claim—which we shall undertake to support in subsequent

[25]This fact has been clearly established by E. E. Aubrey, *Present Theological Tendencies* (New York, 1936), pp. 25–29.

[26]For a clear acknowledgment of this fact, *see* A. C. McGiffert, *Christianity as History and Faith,* Chap. v; and Shailer Mathews, *The Faith of Modernism,* pp. 180–181.

chapters of this study—that contemporary liberalism as a creed is basically outmoded, and must therefore be critically reconsidered and revised. This means, to be sure, that the theological roots of liberal Protestant nurture must also be re-examined and reconstructed.

CHAPTER TWO

BEYOND THE SOCIAL-GOSPEL IDEA
OF THE KINGDOM OF GOD

AMONG AMERICAN liberal Protestants, the Kingdom of God is a much-used term. It has been especially popular with those liberals who have concerned themselves with the social interpretation of the gospel. "To those whose minds live in the social gospel," said Walter Rauschenbusch in 1917, "the kingdom of God is a dear truth."[1]

The idea of the Kingdom of God is a truth no less dear to modern religious educators. For at no point in American Protestantism, perhaps, has the social gospel rooted itself more deeply than in the modern theory of religious education. It can hardly be denied that the most influential books in the philosophy of religious education during the last generation have all been products, directly or indirectly, of the social-gospel frame of thought.[2] This chapter undertakes to make an analysis of this social theory from the point of view of its underlying doctrine of the Kingdom of God.

An effort was made in the foregoing chapter to show that liberal faith, in the closing years of the past century, became more and more dissatisfied with the idea of an other-worldly Kingdom of God. The concept of the Kingdom of God as

[1] *A Theology for the Social Gospel* (New York, 1917), p. 131.
[2] *See* H. F. Cope, "Twenty Years' Progress in Religious Education," *Religious Education,* XVIII (1923), p. 314.

immanent in the present world-order came to be the ruling idea among Christians of the liberal outlook. Along with this tendency to reject an other-worldly notion of the Kingdom also went a tendency to repudiate an individualistic idea of the Kingdom. The idea of the Kingdom on earth and the idea of the Kingdom as social have thus mutually reinforced each other in the rise of religious liberalism. This general mode of thought became basic in the doctrine of Christian nurture from the very beginning of the present century.[3] The Kingdom of God became the ruling concept in religious education as in liberal thought generally, and the new content of the Kingdom was derived from its emphasis upon an earthly Kingdom on the one hand and upon a social Kingdom on the other.

1. The Kingdom as "the Democracy of God"

THAT THE Kingdom of God on earth is construable in terms of an ideal social order has been an implicit or explicit assumption of religious liberalism in America for many years.[1] To describe the nature of this new order the most common term to be used has been democracy. Perhaps this was inevitable in the American scene. In any event, democracy became the most dynamic category by which to interpret

[3]Cf. George A. Coe, *The Religion of a Mature Mind* (New York, 1902), pp. 161–171.

[1]See Lyman Abbott, *The Evolution of Christianity* (New York, 1892), pp. 173–202, 258; Washington Gladden, *Ruling Ideas of the Present Age* (New York, 1895), Chaps. II, III, pp. 289–293; Shailer Mathews, *The Social Teachings of Jesus* (New York, 1897), Chap. III; A. C. McGiffert, *Christianity as History and Faith,* ed. A. C. McGiffert, Jr. (New York, 1934), Chap. XXVIII; Walter Rauschenbusch, *A Theology for the Social Gospel* (New York, 1917), Chap. XIII; George A. Coe, *A Social Theory of Religious Education* (New York, 1917).

the nature of the ideal social community. The first World War served only to enhance the value of this term, since the professed purpose of that conflict was to establish democracy universally. In the heat of conflict, Shailer Mathews expressed the prevailing mood: "It fires our hearts with more than a reasoned conviction that democracy is God's will."[2] In this climate of opinion, it was natural to say that only in democracy could God fully unveil himself to the world. Assuming ourselves to be a democracy, there seemed to be no incongruity in implying that God had therefore manifested His will more completely to Americans. "Because we are Christians," continued Mathews, "we feel in our national life the uplift of the divine presence."[3]

Under the sway of this general outlook it might be supposed that democracy and the Kingdom of God would be envisaged from almost a single perspective. In any case, that is what in effect did happen during the first quarter of the present century. No one did more to stimulate this trend of thought in the theory of Christian nurture than George A. Coe. At numerous points in his long and influential list of writings he has envisaged ideal democracy and the Kingdom of God from a single perspective. Nowhere has he done this with greater force and clarity than in his *A Social Theory of Religious Education,* first published in 1917.[4] Through this book as a whole, says Coe, "there runs a conviction that within Protestantism there is, or is coming to be, a distinctive religious principle, that of a divine-human industrial democracy."[5]

[2]*Patriotism and Religion* (New York, 1918), p. 133.
[3]*Loc. cit.*
[4]By common consent this has been the most influential book in the philosophy of twentieth-century religious education.
[5]*A Social Theory of Religious Education,* p. viii.

It is this conviction that prompts Coe to identify democracy, conceived in terms of a divine-human society, with the Kingdom of God. He therefore substitutes the term "democracy of God" for the biblical phrase "kingdom of God." He does this, he explains, not with the idea of substituting a new social principle, but in order to bring out more clearly what Jesus really meant when he made reference to the Kingdom of God.[6] The goal of Christian nurture thus becomes: "Growth of the young toward and into mature and efficient devotion to the democracy of God, and happy self-realization therein."[7]

This statement of the aim of Christian education contains many elements of great importance, but in this connection we shall confine our attention to what Coe means by the term "democracy of God." No inclusive explanation of it is given at any one point in this book. If, however, one analyzes the discussion as a whole, two basic ideas emerge. One is the idea that the democracy of God involves a universal society of persons, and the other is that ethical love is the creative motive of that society. One of these relates to the form of democracy, the other to its dynamic. Stated briefly, the democracy of God connotes a universal fellowship ruled by the law of love. Each of these two ideas involves, in turn, a twofold aspect, one of which is human and the other divine. A democracy of God signifies therefore a divine-human society whose dynamic is divine-human love.

This concept of the content of the Christian gospel became basic in the thought of Coe long before he brought out this work on the social theory of religious nurture. Germs of it were active in his mental processes before the advent of

[6]*Ibid.*, p. 54.   [7]*Ibid.*, p. 55.

the twentieth century.[8] As early as 1907 he was able to express his concept of the Kingdom of God in a very suggestive fashion. The Kingdom, he wrote, "is primarily the fellowship of all who make love the principle of their life, a fellowship that includes both God and men, both this life and that which is to come."[9] It is this idea of the Kingdom that underlies his social theory of religious education. What he in 1907 spoke of as the Kingdom of God, he in 1917 called the democracy of God.[10] Two different terms are used, but they both seem to signify much the same thing.[11]

Apparently Coe did not intend to introduce a new principle when he decided to make use of the term democracy in which to convey Jesus' conception of the Kingdom of God. Nevertheless, a new social and religious consciousness had dawned among Protestant liberals, and the deeper meaning of the Kingdom, it was felt, could be adequately expressed only in terms of the ideal of democracy. The new term thus served to clarify, rather than to create, the new meanings and values that had emerged in modern culture. Coe's democratic interpretation of the Kingdom was an integral phase of this changed outlook on both religion and society. A

[8]Cf. Coe, "My Own Little Theatre," in *Religion in Transition,* ed. Vergilius Ferm (New York, 1937), pp. 107–113.

[9]"The Content of the Gospel Message to Men of To-day," in *The Materials of Religious Education: Papers and Proceedings of the Fourth General Convention of the Religious Education Association,* Rochester, New York, February 5–7 (Chicago, 1907), p. 77.

[10]As far back as 1908 Coe said in an address before the Religious Education Association: "As far as American religion has a special character of its own—and I believe it has a very special character— democracy is the mark of it. We are striving after a democratic God." "The Place of the Religious Education Association in the Life of the Nation," in *Education and National Life* (Chicago, 1908), p. 91.

[11]With the exception that by 1917 Coe had already ceased to lay much emphasis on what he in his earlier definition of the Kingdom refers to as the "life to come."

growing democratic experience in Church and State expressed itself most naturally in a democratic doctrine of the Kingdom and of Christian nurture.

That this idea of the Kingdom of God has profoundly influenced the nature, presuppositions, and content of modern Christian nurture is becoming increasingly clear. That it has also enriched the educational content of the contemporary Church at many points can hardly be denied by those who are acquainted with developments since the advent of the present century. These gains should be cherished and stubbornly defended against those who would destroy democratic values in both the Church and the State. A successful defense of these values can be made, however, only if we recognize promptly and adequately that the socio-democratic orientation of the Kingdom of God has also obscured certain aspects of the faith by which vital Christian nurture lives.

2. The Kingdom: Anthropocentric or Theocentric?

WE HAVE already pointed out that the Kingdom of God is for Coe a fellowship which includes both a divine and a human aspect. Yet when he elaborates the meaning of the Kingdom it is usually the divine side that he leaves obscure or at least undeveloped. On the other hand, his exposition of the Kingdom on its social or human side is clear and vigorous; and he emphasizes it in all of his more influential works. He seems thus to agree with an opinion expressed by Henry Churchill King at the opening of the twentieth century: "The first and foremost, the constant, the last, and the greatest study of the theologian must be of persons and of personal relations."[1]

[1]*Reconstruction in Theology* (New York, 1901), p. 234.

In his concern with the Kingdom as a society of persons Coe, of course, has not intended to ignore the divine element. For on his view of an immanent God, one cannot truly experience human fellowship without at one and the same time experiencing the divine as well as the human. Here again Coe and King appear to be in agreement. The divine and the human are so intermeshed, says King, that every human relation, when truly fulfilled, not only throws light on the divine, but involves an actual experience of the divine.[2] It is for this reason that King lays so much stress on what he calls "reverence for personality."[3] It is on this basis also that Coe regards respect for personality as the most creative principle of Christian education.

In light of the growth of this tendency of thought it can be seen why the emphasis upon human personality has come to be so dominant in the liberal church. No doubt the advocates of the "personality principle" have conceived themselves to be true to the Christian meaning of the Kingdom of God. Nevertheless, there is reason to believe that the personality principle, as it has been developed in modern religious thought, has not preserved adequately the theocentric nature of the Kingdom. As a result, the Kingdom of God has been distorted, in effect, into an anthropocentric kingdom.

The theory of liberal nurture has shared in this distortion. This distortion, however, is not peculiar to religious education, and upon the religious educator must not be saddled the sole responsibility for obscuring the theocentric orientation of the Kingdom. As a matter of fact, religious education

[2]*Ibid.*, pp. 42–47; 169–175. For a more complete development of this point of view, *see* his *The Moral and Religious Challenge of Our Times* (New York, 1911).

[3]*The Moral and Religious Challenge of Our Times,* Chap. 1.

is the fruit of a distorting process that had been long operative in American religious thought. Nevertheless, certain
elements of modern thought became so uniquely blended in
twentieth-century religious education as to make this movement a strong exponent of the anthropocentric idea of the
Kingdom. A major element in this anthropocentric trend
grows out of the fact that religious education has been greatly
influenced by the theory of public education. Religious education has two roots, one root being modern education and
the other modern religion. The term "religious education"
is itself a reflection of this twofold rootage.

At the dawn of the present century there arose a distinct
feeling in America that religion and education had, for one
reason or another, drifted so far apart as to weaken both,
and by reason of that fact were endangering the spiritual
foundations of civilization. The Religious Education Association, for example, arose in 1903 largely to bring the educational forces and the religious forces into a closer working
unity. At its third annual convention in Boston in 1905, the
Association stated its threefold purpose thus: "To inspire
the educational forces of our country with the religious ideal;
to inspire the religious forces of our country with the educational ideal; and to keep before the public mind the ideal
of religious education, and the sense of its need and value."[4]
In this statement of purpose is a clear recognition of the fact
that religion and education must reinforce each other in the
development of a rich and enduring culture.

In an effort to bring about this unity religious education
has drawn heavily upon the theory of modern education.

[4]*The Aims of Religious Education: Proceedings of the Third Annual Convention of the Religious Education Association,* Boston, February 12–16, 1905, p. 474.

This fact led Shailer Mathews to remark in 1927 that religious education had become little more than public education fitted out in a Prince Albert coat.[5] While this is an exaggeration, it yet contains the truth that religious educators have been deeply influenced by the general theory of the state school. This is particularly true of those religious educators who have sought to blend the democratic theory of education and the democratic theory of the Kingdom of God. In this blending process it cannot be doubted that John Dewey's humanitarian theory of democracy has had great influence.[6]

In light of this background, it is not hard to see why the educational theory of the liberal church was given a strong tendency toward an anthropocentric idea of the Kingdom of God. But in order to show the process by which this happened, it is necessary to examine specific tendencies of recent religious thought. What particular tendencies, then, reflect this humanitarian doctrine of the Kingdom? We shall confine our discussion to three types of tendency.

(a) The first of these grows out of the emphasis that has been placed on the principle of the value of persons. Modern theology—especially the Ritschlian type—has made the idea of the infinite worth of persons a basic element of the Christian faith. According to Ritschl, Jesus understood the Kingdom of God to mean "the organization of humanity through

---

[5]"Let Religious Education Beware!" *The Christian Century*, XLIV (1927), pp. 362-368.

[6]In the foreword to his *Social Theory*, p. x, George A. Coe writes: "Any reader who is familiar with present movements in educational thought will perceive, as this work proceeds, how much I owe to writers who have in mind the public school rather than religious education. I am indebted most of all to John Dewey, who is foremost among those who have put education and industrial democracy into a single perspective."

action inspired by love."[7] Implicit in his analysis of Jesus' concept of the Kingdom is the doctrine of the supreme worth of persons. The Ritschlian Harnack gave this doctrine explicit attention. In his *What Is Christianity?* he took the position that the message of Jesus could be most clearly grasped when it is conceived in terms of the Fatherhood of God and the infinite value of the human soul.[8] On this view of Jesus' teaching, says Harnack, one is able to establish the Christian principle of the "transvaluation of values."[9]

This emphasis on the value of persons has become almost an obsession with the modern religious educator. Being his stock-in-trade, he injects the theme into practically every educational discussion. Whether he undertakes to express the nature of the Kingdom of God or that of democracy, he is almost certain to come round sooner or later—and usually sooner—to the "personality principle." This is especially true of those Christian liberals who stress what they term "democratic religion."[10] Yet this interest in democratic religion has tended in some circles to obscure the divine ground of human value. This may be seen in two types of emphasis in modern religious thought. One of these is the emphasis on what is spoken of as the principle of the "infinite value" of human personality. In support of this principle appeal has often been made to the Biblical passage, "What shall it profit a man if he shall gain the whole world and lose his own

[7]*The Christian Doctrine of Justification and Reconciliation* (2nd ed., Eng. tr., Edinburgh, 1902), p. 12.

[8]*What Is Christianity?* (Eng. tr., New York, 1903), p. 68. For a more detailed exposition of this idea of the gospel, *see* pp. 68–76.

[9]*Ibid.,* p. 73.

[10]For a suggestive exposition of democratic religion as over against individualist and imperialist types of religion, *see* W. A. Brown, *Imperialistic Religion and the Religion of Democracy* (New York, 1923), Chap. v.

life?" It is clearly loose exegesis, however, to say that this passage supports the idea of the infinite value of personality. From this text one may claim only that persons are of more worth than the "whole world." As between the world of things and the world of persons, persons are, to be sure, superior in value to things. One may ask, "Of how much more value is a man than a sheep?" without implying that man is a being of absolute worth. From the standpoint of Christian faith there seems to be no ground on which to say that human personality is a value of "final worth."[11] For to ascribe final worth to persons is in effect to deny Christianity's claim that man is a contingent creature. The secular humanist may legitimately attribute final or absolute value to persons; for to him there is no being beyond man himself. Christian faith, however, cannot do this without sacrificing an essential element in its doctrine of man. For it is the Christian faith that man is a theonomous being. This means man is not autonomous or final, but derives his meaning and value from his relation to God, the highest value. When, therefore, the principle of respect for personality is carried to the length of endowing persons with supreme worth, then the Christian conception of human value is perverted. The way is then opened for a subtle deification of humanity. And this, in turn, starts a trend toward the kingdom of man as a substitute for the Kingdom of God.

There is a second type of emphasis that likewise threatens to obscure the divine ground of the value of persons. It arises out of a certain type of social interpretation of the origin and nature of personality. Under the influence of social psy-

---

[11]Anders Nygren goes so far as to say "that the idea of the infinite value of the human soul is not a basic Christian idea at all." *Agape and Eros* (Eng. tr., London, 1932), p. 55.

chology, it has become a commonplace to conceive the emergence of personal selves in terms of social interaction. Self-consciousness and social consciousness, it is said, not only arise together; the experience of being a self is *per se* an experience of other selves.[12] Thus "my self-consciousness is social consciousness."[13] Some thinkers, following George H. Mead, even go so far as to say that the self is purely the result of an interactive process between the human organism and the natural world.

This tendency of thought has greatly influenced the social theory of liberal religious education. With it there has emerged a definite tendency to equate the value of man with his value to humanity. Since persons are said to be the locus of supreme value, and since values are *per se* social values, human value lies in the fact that man is a member of the Great Society. Personality is thus sacred to society. Persons not only realize themselves in and through society; the Great Society is itself the norm by which their value must finally be measured. But when the values of persons are thus measured exclusively in social or human terms, it is obvious that persons lose their transcendent meaning and value. With their transcendent value denied or obscured, the way is therefore opened to subordinating persons to whatever social system may become dominant. It is thus no surprise that the complete socialization of human value should be followed by some sort of dictatorship, whether of the Left or of the Right.

(*b*) There is a second tendency that is closely related to the first. It is the tendency to identify religion with the process of the discovery of the ethical meaning and worth of persons. Since persons are of supreme worth, the edu-

[12]*Cf.* G. A. Coe, *Psychology of Religion* (Chicago, 1916), p. 250.
[13]*Ibid.*, p. 252.

cative process in religion must, it is said, center in the experience of self-realizing persons.

In his *Psychology of Religion,* George A. Coe writes: "Religion is the discovery of persons."[14] In the history of religion, it is said, man has gradually and progressively discovered himself. Self-discovery is inseparably social, since persons realize themselves only in and through social interaction. The mark of the growth of religion and of the discovery of man alike is thus social integration. The wider the social integration, the higher will be religion and the more meaningful will be man. The process of social integration is dynamic and never stops, else religion becomes arrested and thereby obstructs cultural and ethical evolution. The creative center of this process of continuous integration is man in process of personal-social self-realization. Man is discovering himself, it is said, through the reintegration of his wants in terms of personal-social self-realization. "And this is religion."[15]

Involved in this view that religion is the discovery of persons is another idea that must not be overlooked. It is the idea that, in the order of religious apprehension, man first discovers fresh values in human relations and then projects them into the nature of ultimate reality.[16] Thus new insights into the ethical character of God are dependent upon new and more radical adventures in the ethical relations of persons. Harrison S. Elliott implies this when he says that "God is found as individuals find themselves in the great coöperative enterprises for human progress."[17] A psychological analysis of the history of religious evolution is supposed to support the claim that fresh insight into the character of God

[14]*Ibid.,* p. 240.   [15]*Ibid.,* p. 244.   [16]*Ibid.,* pp. 237–245.
[17]*Bearing of Psychology upon Religion* (New York, 1916), p. 75.

follows rather than precedes cultural evolution. Faith in God "is social valuation asserting itself as objectively valid."[18] "It is a perfectly safe assertion," says Coe, "that men first attributed ethical love to the divine being after they had experienced it among themselves."[19]

Now it is our claim that this general emphasis has tended to obscure the theocentric meaning of the Kingdom. When religion is conceived as the process of the discovery of persons, it inevitably follows that the educational process of the Church will concern itself with the interhuman relations of persons. From this it follows logically that the integrating core of the curriculum of the Church will be "social relations."[20] It is usually assumed, of course, that the divine is in some sense immanent in these social relations, and that under certain conditions of fellowship the qualities of the divine will emerge.[21]

But as a matter of fact this mode of approach has not resulted in a primary emphasis on God at all. On the contrary, persons as an interactive community have been made central. There is an implied assumption that contact with God may be made only indirectly through social relations. Thus Edwin E. Aubrey comments in respect of a conference of religious educators: "It was curious that no reference was made in the discussions of religious education to the problem of man's direct contact with God; and the tendency was to identify this in some way with social contacts."[22]

[18]Coe, *Psychology of Religion,* p. 242.

[19]*What Is Christian Education?* (New York, 1929), p. 76.

[20]William C. Bower, *The Curriculum of Religious Education* (New York, 1925), p. 234.

[21]*Ibid.,* p. 237.

[22]"A Theology Relevant to Religious Education," *Religious Education,* xxxiv (1939), p. 201.

Any such view involves distinct peril for Christian faith, and consequently peril for Christian nurture. To be sure, one's contact with God is stimulated and enriched by social community. But if any one should assume that there can be no sort of contact with God except through other persons, then he assumes something which involves an infinite regress of relations which either denies or obscures the reality of God. Any such view, furthermore, involves a denial that man may experience contact with God in and through the processes of the world of nature. It involves also a denial of God as transcendent of human creatures.

There is a further weakness in the view that religion is primarily the discovery of persons. Not only does it tend to equate the experience of God with the experience of social community, but it tends to identify experience of God with a certain mode or quality of human striving. In his autobiographical essay, George A. Coe says: "Religion is not something added to the functions that make a man a man, but something already within these functions *when they are intensely pursued*. To be religious is as natural as it is to be in dead earnest about anything."[23]

Implicit in this point of view are two dangers. The first is religious subjectivity. The principle of intensity of effort contains in itself no criterion as to what makes any particular function or experience religious. For one may pursue energetically any sort of goal, whether good or bad. Even if one should combine the principle of intensity of pursuit with the process of the discovery of persons, the key to what makes a given function religious is still subjective and obscure.

[23]"My Own Little Theatre," in *Religion in Transition*, p. 106. Italics added. For a similar point of view voiced by a group of prominent religious educators, *see* W. C. Bower, *et al.*, "The Nature and Function of Religion," *Religious Education*, xxxi (1936), p. 97.

The second danger is activism. From the view that religion is a quality of experience that arises through intense effort, it follows that Christian nurture will concern itself less with the Divine Initiative than with human striving. This is precisely what has happened. The idea of progressive religious education is rooted in the assumption that religious experience emerges where self-realizing persons creatively adjust themselves to their natural and social world. On this basis the creative center is located in self-striving man, who is conceived as the builder of the Kingdom. To be sure, the reality of the Kingdom of God is not denied; nevertheless, it is regarded as chiefly the result of human achievement. Thus the source of the Kingdom has become in effect anthropocentric.

Before leaving this topic we must examine the notion that persons first achieve insights and values within human relations and only thereafter project them into the character of God.[24] Particular values attributed to God are, in this view, a derivative of social achievement and evaluations. The history of religion shows new conceptions of God emerging in the course of social evolution. It is assumed, therefore, that new apprehensions of the divine follow social re-evaluation of values. Thus it follows that new values in God await new valuations among men. A new insight into God's nature cannot be had, it is said, "until we experience a new social order in operation."[25]

[24]*Cf*. Charles A. Ellwood, *The Reconstruction of Religion* (New York, 1922), pp. 39–42, 125–126.

[25]"My Own Little Theatre," in *Religion in Transition,* p. 109. In his *What Is Christian Education?,* p. 268, Coe says: "We ourselves must make a new demonstration of ethical love in human relations, or else lose our faith in God."

We must frankly question the basic assumption that underlies this notion. That the history of religion supports it seems doubtful. To be sure, the rise of religion does reflect changing conceptions of God. For example, God was conceived as a tribal being at one stage of Israel's culture and as a universal being at another. But does this fact warrant one in assuming that a higher estimate of the character of God could not arise until antecedent reconstruction in the social culture had first achieved it? Apparently not. For in that case the belief that God desired universal peace, for example, would have been inconceivable in the days of Micah, since at that time a world society had not yet realized universal peace.

There is, to be sure, a vital connection between human relations and fellowship with God. An ancient Christian writer reminds us of this fact, when he says: "He that sayeth, I love God, and hateth his brother, is a liar." This passage, however, lends no support to the notion that the quality of love must first be achieved exclusively in human relations before it can be applied to the nature of God. Indeed, great religious prophets have always transcended the experiences and insights of the social culture in which they grew up.[26] It is unrealistic to assume that the religious insights of an Isaiah, for example, were merely social achievements and evaluations projected into the character of the universe. Isaiah's vision had crucial consequences for the social scene, but that vision did not itself grow out of an already reconstructed social order. In his experience of a holy God, Isaiah recognized that he was a man of unclean lips, and it was on the basis of this experience that he was

[26]*Cf.* Henri Bergson, *The Two Sources of Morality and Religion* (Eng. tr., London, 1935), p. 67.

able to make the social evaluation, "and I dwell among a people of unclean lips."

The point of this should be clear. Those who would have us believe that new insights into the divine nature can be achieved only after they have been realized within human relations, not only deny the most characteristic aspect of prophetic religion; they invert the order of moral insight. They thus weaken religious insight at the very point where they seek to awaken it. It cannot be denied, of course, that social crises precipitate serious reflection, and that this mood predisposes the sensitive ear to hear "what the Spirit saith unto the churches." Nor can it be denied that man's highest ideals serve as a medium through which to envisage the moral character of God. Such truths may be recognized, however, without one's needing to conclude that new religious insight can emerge only from an already achieved new social order.

(c) A third sort of tendency that we shall examine briefly is connected with the idea of sovereignty. Either explicitly or implicitly the value of persons is usually assumed to be the ultimate ground and dynamic of the democratic state. We have already seen that liberal religion also makes the value of persons one of its most creative principles. Thus both democracy and religion are one in emphasizing the essential dignity and worth of persons. In this respect, at least, these two interests are reciprocal in modern culture.[27]

It is of interest to observe that, concurrent with this emphasis on the dignity and worth of persons, there has been a tendency to modify the idea of divine sovereignty. Demo-

[27]In his *Reconstruction of Religion*, Charles A. Ellwood says: "Modern democracy is essentially a movement to realize the ideals of social religion; and all genuine social religion is necessarily a religion of democracy." P. 249.

cratic religion, it has been urged, cannot fulfil its true meaning until it has brought about a democratic theology.[28] "Must
not Christians," asks George A. Coe, "think of God as being
within human society in the democratic manner of working,
helping, sacrificing, persuading, co-operating, achieving?"[29]

This point of view finds a significant application in
Bower's theory of religious education. In his view God is
not only experienced in the fellowship of group participation; God is Himself a democratic sharer in the group
process. "As a member of the community," says Bower, "God
shares in the ideals, purposes, and decisions of the group,
as do its other members. Contrariwise, the decisions of the
group are made with reference to what are believed to be
the ideals and purposes of the Supreme Member. In such a
situation prayer as communion between himself and God
becomes as normal as communion between himself and
other members of the group."[30]

This democratic interpretation of God's relation to men
has served important ends. As over against a concept of God
as one who stands aloof from the human struggle, who
rules by arbitrary decree, and who manipulates persons as
mechanical puppets, the democratic idea of God is certainly
to be preferred. But insofar as the democratic idea of God
obscures the fact that God is wholly sovereign in His Kingdom, and that man is utterly dependent upon God, it must
be regarded as defective. There is reason to believe that the
true meaning of divine sovereignty has been obscured in

[28]"The next step in the development of an ethical theology," wrote
Gerald B. Smith in 1913, "must be the translation of the categories
of divinity into terms compatible with democratic ethics." *Social
Idealism and the Changing Theology* (New York, 1913), p. 228.

[29]*A Social Theory of Religious Education,* p. 55.

[30]*The Curriculum of Religious Education,* p. 237. Italics added.

modern culture. The root of this obscuration may be found in modern religious thought as well as in democratic theory.

It is generally agreed that the locus of sovereignty in modern political democracy is in "we, the people." In the democratic state, says Coe, the sovereign "is neither a god nor the surrogate of a god. . . . The sovereign is just ourselves when we co-operatively insist upon providing for ourselves what we want."[31] And this "is the ultimate meaning of the separation of the church from the state."[32] The implication of this point of view almost startles one. It seems to say in effect that whenever persons jointly determine to pursue their self-chosen ends, there is no sovereignty beyond themselves by which they need feel bound. Human sovereignty, in this view, is primordial and self-sufficient. "Actual, living sovereignty . . . is wholly within the flux of experience; . . . it is in continuous creation and re-creation, even within ourselves."[33]

If this be the ultimate meaning of the separation of the democratic state from the Church, then it cannot be doubted that the theory of the modern democratic state does obscure the truth of divine sovereignty. If the Kingdom of God be truly sovereign over every social community, the democratic state included, then it cannot be admitted that divine sovereignty is wholly within the flux of human experience. On the other hand, when the ultimate meaning of sovereignty is wholly identifiable with the inner meaning of the fellowship of persons, the only sovereignty that can be recognized is human sovereignty.

Liberal Christianity has also had a part in obscuring the principle of the sovereignty of God in His Kingdom. This

[31]*Educating for Citizenship* (New York, 1932), p. 143.
[32]*Loc. cit.*   [33]*Ibid.*, p. 186.

is reflected, for example, in the liberal's emphasis on divine immanence. If religious orthodoxy sometimes tended to deny all continuity between God and man, liberalism has tended to overemphasize continuity. The doctrine of immanence afforded liberal religious thought a basis upon which to conceive of man as being essentially divine in the depth of his being, and therefore as containing within himself the essential principle of his own worth and government. In this lies the main source of human dignity and of self-determination.

Along with this emphasis upon human dignity there has been a continuous protest against any notion of an absolute power and value, not less in the realm of religion than in that of political life. The demand for a limited ruler in state has had its counterpart in a demand for a limited God.[34] That movement in modern culture that swept out the doctrine of the divine right of kings was but one phase of a social process that swept in the era of the "rights of man." In a notable presidential address before the Religious Education Association in 1919, A. C. McGiffert said: "A religion that is to promote and sustain democracy must first of all be a religion of faith in man."[35] The logic of this emphasis he brings out in that same message: "Of course education in a democracy should not be such as to encourage the delusive belief in supernatural agencies and dependence upon them, but it should be such as to convince everybody that things can be controlled and moulded by the power of man."[36] Democracy "demands a God with whom men may coöperate, not to whom they must submit."[37] This conception of

[34]*Cf.* Francis J. McConnell, *Democratic Christianity* (New York, 1919), p. 4.
[35]"Democracy and Religion," *Religious Education,* xiv (1919), p. 158.
[36]*Ibid.,* p. 157.   [37]*Ibid.,* p. 161.

democratic religion tends to undermine the meaning of divine sovereignty. In effect it reverses the relation of God and man. The creature under the Kingdom thus becomes the master over the Kingdom.

3. The Kingdom on Earth

THE TENDENCY in the social theory of Christian nurture to assimilate the Kingdom of God to an anthropocentric fellowship has been an integral part of another trend to equate the Kingdom with an ideal earthly society. This latter tendency had become a basic aspect of the social gospel before the advent of the twentieth-century movement in liberal nurture. Thus Josiah Strong, in 1893, wrote: "Revelation certainly teaches that final earthly society is to be perfect . . . free from all taint of evil."[1] This optimistic temper spread rapidly during the next decade. Only a year before the first World War broke out, Washington Gladden prophesied: "People will be living in heaven right here in the Scioto Valley."[2] The social theory of religious education thus inherited a strong bias toward a this-worldly doctrine of the Kingdom of God.

In this emphasis religious education of the present century has actively participated, with the result that it, no less than other processes in the liberal church, has had a definite part in obscuring the essential distinction between the Kingdom of God and every form of earthly society. This has reflected itself in two different types of emphasis.

(a) The first concerns Jesus' idea of the Kingdom of God. Throughout the early years of the present century New

[1] *The New Era, or the Coming Kingdom* (New York, 1893), p. 20.
[2] *Present Day Theology* (Columbus, 1913), p. 120.

Testament thought, based on historical criticism, really believed that Jesus conceived the Kingdom in terms of a perfected earthly society. Thus in 1897 Shailer Mathews boldly stated that "by the Kingdom of God Jesus meant an ideal . . . social order."[3]

Many other leaders of the social-gospel movement championed this point of view during the next twenty years. Of this group, Charles Foster Kent deserves special attention, since he, like Mathews, was both a gospel critic and a leader in religious education. Kent published his well-known book, *The Social Teachings of the Prophets and Jesus,* just as America was entering the World War of 1914–18. In this he expresses the opinion that Jesus was "impelled by a social aim and plan" from the moment that he left home.[4] He thus taught the Lord's Prayer as a means of keeping before his disciples the goal of "a perfect social order," the Kingdom on earth.[5] Jesus not only possessed a "social philosophy," but he entered Capernaum with a definite plan to organize "a fraternal community" in which to demonstrate the social effectiveness of that philosophy.[6] From Capernaum Jesus would be able to spread the ideals of his social fraternity into all parts of Palestine.[7] His sharp criticism of Chorazin and Bethsaida was the result of a bitter sense of the failure of his social project.[8]

In the light of later gospel research, this sounds fantastic;[9]

[3]*The Social Teachings of Jesus* (New York, 1897), p. 54. In his autobiography, *New Faith for Old* (New York, 1936), p. 120, Mathews writes: "So far as I know this book was the first of its kind in English in its field."

[4]New York, 1917, p. 186.

[5]*Ibid.,* p. 279.   [7]*Ibid.,* pp. 187–189.
[6]*Ibid.,* pp. 182, 278 ff.   [8]*Ibid.,* p. 195.

[9]*See,* for example, Henry J. Cadbury, *The Peril of Modernizing Jesus* (New York, 1937).

but it was taken seriously by Kent and many others of his generation. The social theory of modern religious education is the fruit of this interpretation of the Christian gospel. Furthermore, this idea of the social gospel continues to exercise an influence in certain circles, although it is stated more cautiously than it was by Kent. In one of his more recent books, *Religion and the Good Life,* William C. Bower says Jesus "envisioned a reconstructed and ideal social order which he called the kingdom of God."[10] The most basic aspect of Jesus' teaching, he contends, centered in "social idealism." Jesus therefore "spoke of this idealized society as the kingdom of God."[11] More recently Theodore G. Soares expressed essentially the same point of view.[12]

If the transcendent nature of the Kingdom had not been obscured, it would have been difficult for the liberal religious educator to identify the Kingdom of which Jesus spoke with any sort of ideal social order. But once the true character of the Kingdom faded from experience, it was only natural that Jesus should be called "the most thorough-going democrat"[13] and his Kingdom be conceived as an ideal democracy on earth. In this view it is not hard to see why democratic nurture and Christian nurture should have been fused to the extent that, for many left-wing liberals, they became but two different names for essentially the same thing. If there remained any difference it lay chiefly in the fact that Christian nurture was expected to go the second mile in social radicalism.[14]

[10]New York, 1933, p. 79.   [11]*Ibid.,* p. 92.
[12]"Personality Development and the God Experience," *Religious Education,* xxxi (1936), p. 120.
[13]Kent, *op. cit.,* p. 254.
[14]*Cf.* G. A. Coe, "What Is Religious Education?" *Religious Education,* xviii (1923), p. 95.

Against this tendency to obscure the distinction between the Kingdom of God and any given social order, Christian nurture is forced to protest if it is to serve as a vital agency of faith in the Church of tomorrow. It must recognize that the Kingdom of which Jesus spoke will always be a transcendent reality never to be fully translated into the relative forms of human culture. Christian faith must therefore sharply protest any tendency to equate the Kingdom of God with democracy or with any other type of social order.

The point of view advanced here does not, however, imply that the Kingdom is a purely otherworldly reality. For Christian nurture, if it apprehends the true nature of the Kingdom, cannot isolate itself from the struggles of human history. While no empirical social order can be normative for the Kingdom, yet history is the scene in which God's Kingdom serves as a reconstructive force. To be sure, Jesus said, "My Kingdom is not of this world"; yet he also said, "The Kingdom is at hand." These two affirmations, taken together, point to the Christian claim that the Kingdom has been revealed in the world, even though the world is not the source and the ultimate goal of it. History is thus the scene of God's redemptive action, and any effort on the part of the Christian educator to retreat from history is in effect to deny the Church's faith in the doctrine of the Incarnation.

Let us recognize ungrudgingly that the exponents of the social-gospel idea of the Kingdom rendered a necessary service at this point. If in some respects their particular theories tended to relax the abiding tension between the world and the Kingdom of God, they yet should be given credit for turning the Church's attention to empirical history as the scene of God's redeeming action. They rightly reacted against that type of orthodoxy which became preoccupied

with salvation in heaven. For them, as Shailer Mathews recently said, the social gospel was "a call and a way to give
salvation on earth."[15] Against an otherworldly faith that said,
"this world is not my home," the new faith said, "this is my
Father's world," and sought to refashion it into what Kent
called "the democracy of Jesus." They were not wrong in
their conviction that the gospel of the Kingdom constituted
a decisive challenge to the social patterns and processes of
human history. They were wrong only insofar as they identified the Kingdom of God with an ideal social order and
thereby obscured the suprasocial meaning of that Kingdom.

(b) There is a second sort of emphasis in social theory,
closely correlated with the first, that reveals the loss of the
basic distinction between the Kingdom of God and an earthly
social order. It lies in the optimistic faith that the Christian
ethic of the Kingdom is immediately applicable to the collective problems of a complex industrial age. Adelaide T.
Case expressed the prevailing assumption of left-wing liberal
religious educators, when, in 1924, she wrote: "In general,
they [liberals] affirm the desirability and the possibility of
operating the political unit, whether large or small, upon the
humanitarian principles of Jesus—with (a) the absence of
economic strife, (b) no race or class privilege, (c) participation in government of all those not physically or mentally
incompetent, and (d) the ruling motive of aggression replaced by that of mutual service."[16]

That such an ideal political society is desirable no one can
deny. Yet to affirm that this radically new social order can
be brought about through the simple and unqualified prac-

[15]*New Faith for Old,* p. 126.
[16]*Liberal Christianity and Religious Education* (New York, 1924),
p. 48.

tice of "the humanitarian principles of Jesus" is sheer romanticism. It fails to see that large-scale political and social
units can never be so completely emancipated from the sins
of class, race, and imperialism as to rise completely above
economic and racial conflict. This sort of optimism could
never have taken possession of the mind of religious liberals
if they had not first lost a realistic experience of the depth
and power of human sin and evil. Reinhold Niebuhr has
expressed the opinion that the liberal Church resorted to the
"simple expedient of denying, in effect, the reality of evil in
order to maintain its hope in the triumph of the ideal of
love" in human social history.[17] Though this is an over-
simplification of the situation, it at least emphasizes the
truth that those who lose sight of the perennial struggle of
the human heart with sin do tend to overestimate the extent
to which the law of love may be made the unqualified instrument of human control.

Another element of romanticism in this general point of
view is the belief that the Christian ethic of the Kingdom of
God may serve as a simple and unqualified alternative to
the political strategies of a relativistic social order. The result
is that the liberal educator not only eviscerates the ethic of
Jesus, but he fails to develop realistic strategies by which to
establish relative justice in a technological civilization. Thus
George A. Coe recently admitted that he did not believe that
he and other middle-class intellectuals and religious liberals
contained within themselves sufficient resources to solve the
problems of a decaying capitalist society. His hope, he said,
is now being placed in the religious and moral resources of
the proletarian masses.[18]

[17]*An Interpretation of Christian Ethics* (New York, 1935), p. 143.
[18]"My Own Little Theatre" in *Religion in Transition*, p. 119.

There seems to be a connection between the liberal's loss of the meaning of the absolute ethic of the Kingdom and his failure to espouse social and political strategies realistic enough to deal with the problems of a technical age. As the ethic of Jesus was relativized, the liberal became not only more optimistic in respect of the coming of the Kingdom, but he also became surer that moralistic persuasion would resolve the conflicts of an industrial society. Although certain left-wing disciples of the social gospel have conceded that under certain circumstances coercion might be necessary, liberals as a rule have put their main trust in what is called the "educational process." At the heart of this faith in education is the assumption that the problems of collective existence can largely be solved by technics of social fellowship and group discussion.[19] Since men ought to love one another, it is thought that they will do so if only they will get around a conference table and really understand one another.

Once the Christian ethic of the Kingdom of God is appreciated in its absolute meaning, it will be evident that the issues of our collective political life will necessitate the development of social technics that are not immediately deducible from that ethic. When once we recognize with C. H. Dodd that we "never do and never can love our enemies, or even our friendly neighbors, as we love ourselves,"[20] then we shall be able to understand why coercion and realistically

[19]Thus Harrison S. Elliott, *Can Religious Education Be Christian?* p. 247, writes: "Even though the method of conference is in dispute because of its prostitution in the Munich Pact and other decisions, it is still the only human alternative to that disastrous use of force, which, while it may temporarily stop the aggressor and secure a modicum of justice for one of the conflicting parties, never solves any problem." *Cf.* pp. 204–218.

[20]*History and the Gospel* (New York, 1938), p. 127.

adjusted balances of power always will be a necessary part
of all strategies of social adjustment.

4. The Process of the Coming Kingdom

THE LIBERAL hope of the Kingdom on earth has been bound
up with a particular idea as to how it· would come. The
liberal Church committed itself wholeheartedly to the idea
of an evolutionary coming of the Kingdom. It is doubtful
if this idea could have arisen if the theory of organic and cultural evolution had not become a fundamental element in
the growth of modern thought. It is also doubtful if it could
have become so influential without the· growth of the idea of
divine immanence. But whatever were the forces at work in
its origin and growth, the evolutionary theory of the coming
of the Kingdom has played a dominant role in the thought
of liberal Protestantism.

As in other aspects of liberal faith, this doctrine of a
growing Kingdom sought and found support in the teachings of Jesus. Gospel critics of the early years of the twentieth
century were as a rule convinced that Jesus believed in the
growth idea of the Kingdom of God. No one, to be sure,
thought that Jesus used the term evolution in his teaching.
Nevertheless, it was held that Jesus did believe the Kingdom
would emerge on earth in terms of an evolutionary process.[1]
Walter Rauschenbusch stated the general notion of many
pre-war liberals when, in 1911, he wrote: "Translate the
evolutionary theories into religious faith, and you have the

---

[1] Cf. Shailer Mathews, *The Social Teachings of Jesus*, p. 203. In
fairness to Mathews, it should be said that in later years he saw and
admitted that Jesus spoke in eschatological rather than in evolutionary terms. *See* his *Jesus on Social Institutions* (New York, 1928), and
New Faith for Old, p. 120.

doctrine of the Kingdom of God."[2] In support of this view-point appeal was usually made to the parables of Jesus, especially the parables of the Leaven and the Mustard Seed.[3]

The twentieth-century educational theory of the liberal Church was given its main impetus by this interpretation of the coming of the Kingdom. If it had not been for this widespread belief in the progressive coming of the Kingdom it is doubtful whether the Church would have turned with such fervent hope to the strategy of evangelism through religious education. The gains made by the Church under this approach to the coming of the Kingdom are widely recognized and should be preserved. It would be a mistake, however, to ignore the limitations in this theory of the coming Kingdom. Whether or not these limitations are necessarily inherent in the doctrine, it can hardly be denied that they have manifested themselves in certain aspects of the theory of religious education. These weaknesses are evident in two tendencies of liberal thought.

(a) One sort of weakness is reflected in the notion that the Kingdom of God is a reality that "grows out of" emerging social experience. Exponents of the idea of an emerging Kingdom are generally monistic in their world-view, and they revolt against all supernaturalistic interpretations of reality.

In recent years no religious educator has been more pro-

---

[2]*Christianizing the Social Order* (New York, 1911), p. 90.

[3]*See* Lyman Abbott, *Christianity and Social Order* (New York, 1896), p. 18; Mathews, *The Social Teachings of Jesus,* p. 205; King, *The Ethics of Jesus* (New York, 1910), pp. 62–64; Francis G. Peabody, *Jesus Christ and the Social Question* (New York, 1900), pp. 101–102, 286; Rauschenbusch, *Christianity and the Social Crisis* (New York, 1907), pp. 59–60; Kent, *The Social Teachings of the Prophets and Jesus,* pp. 275–278; Abbott, *What Christianity Means to Me* (New York, 1921), pp. 176–177.

nounced in this emphasis than William C. Bower.[4] In Bower's view, the values of the Kingdom of God "have not invaded the life of the community from some remote and supernatural realm; they have grown up within the stream of the experience of Christians."[5] On this basis these values would seem to be merely subjective elements of human experience. Since the values of religion "arise within the depths of the social experience," the coming of the Kingdom is considered to be continuous with, and the subjective aspect of, an evolving social culture.[6]

Yet religion, says Bower, exercises a critical and reconstructive function in social culture. But if religion is to function as a critical and creative factor in culture it must be something more than a purely subjective element of that culture. Implied in every act of moral criticism is the principle of moral transcendence. If, therefore, as Bower says, religion does serve as a process of "the cross-criticism" of values, then obviously there is operative in this process an element that transcends those values. Bower is somewhat aware of the problem that this situation presents. Nevertheless, he continues to assume that the problem can be solved in terms of a purely empirical approach to the values of the Kingdom of God.

Our analysis thus reveals the weakness that attends the theory of an "emerging" Kingdom of God. It lies in the tendency to obscure the objective character of the values of

---

[4]*See,* for example, his polemic article, "Points of Tension Between Progressive Religious Education and Current Theological Trends," *Religious Education,* xxxiv (1939), pp. 69–72.

[5]*The Church at Work in the Modern World* (Chicago, 1935), p. 3.

[6]Bower, "Points of Tension Between Progressive Religious Education and Current Theological Trends" in *Religious Education,* xxxiv (1939), p. 170.

the Christian faith. It inclines toward a false identification of religion and culture. Religion thus becomes merely a subjective aspect or quality of social culture. Consequently it inclines one to think that the way to render current religion creative is to unearth the spiritual values that are inherent in contemporary culture. But if a culture has been bereft of its deeper spiritual elements, this offers no solution. When the eighth-century Prophets, for example, sought to create religious vitality, they did not attempt to do this merely by uncovering the spiritual values inherent in their contemporary culture; on the contrary, they brought judgment to bear upon their culture in the name of a sovereign and righteous God. Thus the religious solution to our contemporary culture does not lie merely in uncovering the spiritual elements of that culture. It lies rather in a transcendent experience of the Kingdom of God.

(b) There is another element of weakness that must be indicated in this context. It manifests itself in the form of an overemphasis upon the coming of the Kingdom of God in terms of a process of gradual personal and social growth. It was pointed out in the first chapter how social and religious thought in the closing decades of the last century became preoccupied with the method of gradual evolutionary growth. This tendency became even stronger in the early part of the present century. Those elements in the teaching of Jesus which tended to deny the growth idea of the coming Kingdom of God either were taken to be alien to his thought[7] or they were regarded as of minor importance from the point of view of modern religious faith. Biological and psychologi-

[7] For a brief survey of the recent New Testament research that corrects this non-eschatological point of view, *see* Amos P. Wilder, *Eschatology and Ethics in the Teachings of Jesus* (New York, 1939), Chap. II.

cal studies added to the general drift. On the basis of research into the phenomena of religious experience in childhood and youth, the idea of "normal" became associated with
that type of religious change that was marked by gradual
growth, whereas, by implication, the idea of "abnormal" was
identified with all other modes of religious change.[8] The
same principle was applied to social processes; only those
were considered normal that were marked by change of a
gradual or growthlike sort.

From the perspective of today, this emphasis in liberal
religious nurture reveals itself as the typical fruit of a culture
that was characterized by economic advancement, peaceful
social and political change, and relative freedom from sharp
and sudden crises. Within that context of events, to envisage
change, both social and personal, in terms of a doctrine of
evolutionary growth was a natural reaction of moral and
religious nurture.

Nevertheless, it seems increasingly clear to those who find
themselves confronted with the pressures and crises of the
new era that this growth-theory of social and religious change
must be critically re-evaluated. The social and political patterns of today are shifting rapidly and drastically, and the
element of continuity in social change is far less dominant
than the element of discontinuity. To construe these catastrophic changes within the pattern of social and political
growth would be absurd. For the fact is, western culture is
passing through a crisis the like of which comes only when
civilization is pivoting over from one culture-era to another.

Thus it seems unlikely that the growth-theory of religious
education will be able to produce a sufficiently realistic

[8] *Cf.* E. S. Ames, *The Psychology of Religious Experience* (New
York, 1910), Chap. III.

strategy of change for the new age of crisis. For, in the first place, the growth-theory presupposes a pattern of gradual social change; but the coming era calls for change on a revolutionary scale. In the second place, the growth-theory presupposes peaceful change through moral persuasion; but the prospect for the immediate future, at least, is that coercive force will be used increasingly as an instrument of social control. For these reasons, therefore, the growth-theory will need certain modifications in order to be of service in the catastrophic scene in which mankind is destined to live for many years to come.

CHAPTER THREE

MAN IN CHRISTIAN PERSPECTIVE

EVERY PERIOD of acute social crisis has had the effect, sooner or later, of centering attention upon the fundamental question of man's nature and destiny. The present is no exception to the rule. With the decay of liberal civilization, the rise of new political faiths, and the radical shift in values—all of which mark what Berdyaev has called the "end of our time" —the irrepressible question re-emerges, What is man? The new political faiths that have arisen since the first World War have given answers to this question which essentially contradict the Christian understanding of man. In this there is raised a challenge which the Church cannot evade. Thus it is no surprise that the ecumenical forces at Oxford should have recognized the need for a restatement of the Christian doctrine of man.[1]

A far-reaching reconsideration of this issue needs to be undertaken in America as well as in other parts of the world. Indeed, there is some reason to believe that it needs even more critical attention here than elsewhere. It is true that American religious thought has devoted much study to certain aspects of human personality. In part this was the outgrowth of a growing emphasis in both theology and religious education upon reverence for personality as "the best key for man's discernment of himself, for the interpretation of

[1] Cf. T. E. Jessop, et al., The Christian Understanding of Man (An Oxford Conference Book, Chicago, 1938).

history, and for the understanding of God in all His relations to men."[2] This general idea lies at the root of the liberal movement in Christian nurture.[3] This trend in thought would naturally have the effect of focusing primary attention upon the nature, experience, and activity of persons.

But in spite of this extended study of human nature throughout the period of the present century, it becomes more and more evident that the liberal Church does not possess a realistic understanding of man from the point of view of Christian faith. Thus Willard L. Sperry writes: "Modern Liberalism, whether political or religious, needs nothing so much as a realistic and credible doctrine of man."[4]

Paradoxically, the generation that has been preoccupied with the study of man finds itself in the predicament of discovering that it does not really know man! This is not the place to inquire in detail why liberalism is today without an adequately realistic understanding of man. The causes are no doubt numerous and puzzling. There is, however, one basic reason that must be mentioned here. It lies in the fact that the liberal theory of religious nurture has been dominated by the sciences of psychology, sociology and anthropology.[5] Under the spell of these sciences, religious educators

[2]King, *The Moral and Religious Challenge of Our Times* (New York, 1911), pp. 1–2. *See also Reconstruction in Theology* (New York, 1901), Chap. IX; *Theology and the Social Consciousness* (New York, 1902), Chap. XII; *Rational Living* (New York, 1905), pp. 236–246.

[3]*Cf.* G. A. Coe, *What Is Christian Education?* (New York, 1929).

[4]"Liberalism," *Christendom*, v (1940), p. 185.

[5]Thus Harrison S. Elliott, in his *Can Religious Education Be Christian?* (New York, 1940), says: "The data from the sciences of psychology, sociology and anthropology and from the developments in general education . . . rather than theological conceptions, have been the controlling factors in the development of program and method in religious education." P. 4.

concentrated their attention upon those particular aspects of personality that could be examined within the framework of empirical events. In some circles, furthermore, there was overpreoccupation with relatively narrow units of behavior; with units that could be isolated from their context and objectively examined. The emphasis upon the specific and the concrete, which was inspired by experimental psychology, tended to obscure the meaning of man in his wholeness and in his wider relations. While, to be sure, the social sciences have seen man as a member of group life, they have not undertaken to see man in terms of his ultimate relations.

Thus the net result is that twentieth-century religious education has concerned itself so completely with man in his empirical manifestation that it has tended to obscure, and in some instances to deny, the ultimate ground of human existence. This fact was pointed out by Shailer Mathews when, in 1927, he warned religious educators that they were "in danger of hiding God behind a smoke-screen of psychology."[6] The result of this general tendency is that the Christian perspective of man has been largely neglected.

It is our claim that man, from the Christian point of view, is a theonomous being. That is to say, he is a being who is created "in the image of God." This signifies that man can be truly understood only from the divine perspective.[7] Thus while the sciences of psychology and sociology are indispensable to our total knowledge of man, they do not, as

[6]"Let Religious Education Beware," *The Christian Century* XLIV (1927), p. 362. More recently Mathews wrote: "I cannot help feeling that until religious education passes beyond psychology to religion as a technique of relationship with those cosmic activities which we conceive of as God, it will fail to perform a much-needed function." *New Faith for Old,* p. 251.

[7]This point of view has been most forcefully advanced by Emil Brunner, *Man in Revolt* (Eng. tr., New York, 1939), pp. 102 ff.

sciences, afford us ultimate light on the origin, nature, and destiny of human existence. In this sphere, at least, Christian faith, implemented by theology, has an indispensable word. The discussion that follows thus attempts to understand man in terms of a theocentric frame of reference, and it undertakes to point out some of the more important implications of this perspective for Christian nurture. No attempt is made to deal with every aspect of Christian anthropology. Rather, attention is concentrated on certain particular aspects that seem to be most in need of reconsideration by religious educators at the present time.

1. Man as Creature of God

EVERY THEORY of human origin, whether naturalistic or Christian, views man as emerging in terms of a creative process involving causes that are remote as well as immediate. That is to say, man's emergence in empirical history is somehow connected with a series of events in which some events are more ultimate than others, and which, in some sense, are taken as the primordial "ground" of human existence. Even when all doctrines of "creationism" are disavowed, this remains true. The human mind seems unable to come to rest in terms of a series of causal events of infinite regression.

At this point Christian faith involves a fundamental affirmation. Even though Christianity recognizes the place of empirical factors in the emergence of man, it yet affirms that man has his origin ultimately in the creative action of God, the transcendent ground of all finite being. From the beginning the Christian has said, "It is He that made us, and not

we ourselves." Through the ages Christian faith has un-
waveringly believed that "In Him we live and move and
have our being." Basic in the theory of Christian nurture,
therefore, is the question of the perspective from which an
explanation of the emergence of man should be sought.

It cannot be denied that certain types of left-wing religious
liberalism do undertake to explain man's emergence from a
perspective that falls short of the affirmation of Christian
faith. Those adhering to this general mode of thought may,
in broad terms, be referred to as religious naturalists. They
run all the way from humanistic naturalists who reject the
use of the term God in any form to naturalists who make
use of the term to denote a certain kind of activity, process,
and the like, but who yet stop short of conceiving God as
creative Being. Thus all of them fall short, though in varying degrees, of interpreting man's emergence from the complete perspective of Christian faith. Valuable as their insights
on man may be in certain respects, they nevertheless fail to
see human personality in the full dimension of Christianity.
No attempt can be made in this connection to give a systematic account of their religious philosophy in general.[1] Rather
we shall inspect only that aspect of their thought that bears
directly on the problem of the ultimate root of human personality. Furthermore, we can consider the views of only a
few of the religious naturalists. We have, however, chosen
those whose teachings have been particularly influential in
shaping the thought of contemporary religious education.

America's most distinguished religious naturalist is, of
course, John Dewey. It would be hard to overestimate the

[1] For a brief survey of the religious philosophy of this group of
thinkers, see H. N. Wieman and B. E. Meland, *American Philosophies of Religion* (Chicago, 1936), pp. 251–305.

extent of his influence not only in the sphere of educational theory in general, but in that of religious education. It seems not too much to say that his *Democracy and Education*[2] has been the primary source of many of the most far-reaching ideas in the progressive educational theory of Protestantism. Until Dewey delivered the Terry Lectures at Yale University in 1934[3] he had not published a detailed and systematic statement of his religious faith. Nevertheless, his religious views were widely known long before that time. His interpretation of religion is the logical fruit of his empirical naturalism.[4] Man's emergence he explains in terms of empirical natural forces operating in and through the process of organic and cultural evolution. The basic presupposition of his theory of the genesis of human personality is the continuity of the lower (less complex) and the higher (more complex) forms of life. His idea of continuity means neither "complete rupture" on the one hand nor mere "repetition of identities" on the other.[5] The appearance of human intelligence, however, does not presuppose the operational presence of anything like cosmic mind. Rational operations, he says, "grow out of organic activities."[6] The organism thus becomes a mind through a distinctive mode of interaction with its physical and cultural environment. The transformation of organic behavior into intellectual behavior "is a product of the fact that individuals live in a cultural environment."[7]

[2]New York, 1916.
[3]*A Common Faith* (New Haven, 1934).
[4]For an excellent symposium on Dewey's philosophic position, including an account of his religious thought, *see Library of Living Philosophers,* Vol. 1: *The Philosophy of John Dewey,* ed. Paul A. Schilpp (Northwestern University Press, Evanston and Chicago, 1939).
[5]Dewey, *Logic: The Theory of Inquiry* (New York, 1938), p. 23.
[6]*Ibid.,* p. 19.   [7]*Ibid.,* p. 45.

Strangely enough, Dewey believes that the term God should be retained in the religious interpretation of man. It may, he says, serve to "protect man from a sense of isolation and from consequent despair."[8] In this view the term may be legitimately used to denote, not anything resembling a cosmic creator of man, but "the unity of all ideal ends arousing us to desire and action."[9] It may also be used to signify the *"active* relation between ideal and actual."[10] There is reason, as we shall see, to believe that man needs protection against a sense of isolation and despair, but such protection can hardly come from a God who denotes merely some sort of imaginative reality.

Closely related to the religious thought of Dewey is that of Edward Scribner Ames, who also has had extensive influence in the formation of liberal theory of religious education. His mature point of view is best set forth in *Religion*.[11] In this work Ames takes the position that God denotes neither a being nor existence of any sort, but rather an "order of nature" which includes man and "all the processes of an aspiring social life."[12] Elsewhere he uses the term to signify reality in its ideal aspect.[13] Reality, he admits, is characterized by orderliness, intelligence, and love. When these aspects of reality are idealized, they constitute the God-reality.[14] One must be on his guard, however, not to read into these idealized traits of the world anything that corresponds to a substantial being.

Another influential naturalist is Henry Nelson Wieman. Wieman identifies himself with what he calls "the new

---

[8]*A Common Faith,* p. 53.
[9]*Ibid.,* p. 42.
[10]*Ibid.,* p. 51.
[11]New York, 1929.

[12]*Ibid.,* pp. 176–177.
[13]*Ibid.,* p. 151.
[14]*Ibid.,* pp. 151–156.

naturalism." New naturalism professes to be theistic. Wieman distinguishes his idea of God, however, from all forms of supernaturalism on the one hand and from the Dewey-Ames type of humanism on the other. Supernaturalism identifies God with a reality that is wholly transcendent and humanism with a reality that exists only in ideal. As against the former, he maintains that God "is within the cosmic whole"; and as against the latter, he contends that God signifies a reality other than that which exists in imaginative ideal.[15]

In the opinion of Wieman, any effort to interpret either man's origin or his ultimate goal in terms of Cosmic Being leads to fruitless metaphysical speculation and to religious sterility.[16] Like other naturalists, Wieman prefers to envisage God as "in the actualities of the here and now."[17] God is in the events of the here and now as creative synthesis, or as unlimited connective growth.[18] What is it, then, that generates human personality and brings it to highest fulfilment? The reality which does this "is a very complex and delicate system of connections of mutual control which grows up between the individual psycho-physical-organism and its physical and social environment."[19] This process of mutual growth of creative synthesis is superhuman but it is in no sense a cosmic creator.[20]

For Wieman, linguistic symbols play a basic role in the origin and growth of personality. The sub-human animal is limited to the use of gestures and other signals in his partici-

[15]H. N. Wieman and Walter Horton, *The Growth of Religion* (Chicago, 1938), pp. 340–349, 427–436, 453–458.
[16]*Ibid.*, p. 346.   [18]*Ibid.*, pp. 348, 352–353.
[17]*Ibid.*, p. 347.   [19]*Ibid.*, p. 361.
[20]*Ibid.*, pp. 362–363. *Cf.* H. N. and Regina W. Wieman, *Normative Psychology of Religion* (New York, 1935), pp. 50–59.

pation in the life and behavior of other animals.[21] On the other hand, the human animal is able to communicate with his kind in terms of symbolic-meanings that are freed from concrete contexts. This process of sharing meanings not merely reveals intelligence; it creates the human mind. "The human mind," says Wieman, "is created by the communication of meanings and develops only by such communication."[22]

The more recent thought of William C. Bower seems to fall essentially within the general frame of this sort of religious naturalism. As in the case of naturalists in general, Bower views religion as a functional process in which persons seek a twofold integration: (a) integration within the self and (b) integration with the environing world.[23] The human self is the outgrowth of the interaction of growing selves.[24] What, then, is the nature of the ultimate ground of this twofold process of emerging life? It is "that behavior of the universe which most religious persons represent to themselves in terms of God."[25] More recently Bower has used the term God to signify the creative aspect of "ultimate and comprehending values."[26] But if, as Bower maintains, the "kingdom of values is within the self,"[27] it is clear that value

[21]For a detailed analysis of this process of animal gesture-signals, see George H. Mead, *Mind, Self, and Society* (Chicago, 1934), pp. 117 ff.

[22]*The Growth of Religion*, p. 467. See also p. 354. Wieman seems in this respect to be in basic agreement with Mead, *op. cit.*, pp. 224–226.

[23]*Religion and the Good Life* (New York, 1933), Chaps. VI and XI.

[24]"Points of Tension between Progressive Religious Education and Current Theological Trends," *Religious Education*, XXXIV (1939), p. 168.

[25]*Religion and the Good Life*, p. 45. See also p. 143.

[26]*The Living Bible* (New York, 1936), p. 28. Cf. *Character Through Creative Experience* (Chicago, 1930), pp. 242, 246–249.

[27]*Religion and the Good Life*, p. 217.

is essentially subjective; and on this view the term God can denote no really objective ground of human existence.

All four of these naturalists thus undertake to explain the source of human existence within an empirical perspective. In terms of this perspective, and by critical use of the results of the special sciences, they have shed much light on the growth and behavior of human personality. Any perspective of man that fails to take due account of the tested findings of empirical observation and research must be considered incomplete. That certain types of religious interpretation of man's genesis and development have been defective at this point cannot be denied. This was evident, for example, in the Modernist-Fundamentalist controversy that arose during the decade following the first World War.[28] In its effort to deny attested biological facts with respect to man's animal ancestry, Fundamentalist orthodoxy brought itself into confusion and disrepute.

But if religious orthodoxy has often failed to see man in his empirical perspective, it is also true that naturalistic liberalism has failed to see man in the full dimension of his existence. This is clearly reflected in the thought of such liberals as Dewey, Ames, Wieman, and Bower. Though each of these writers connects the idea of God with the empirical process of human origin and growth, none of them goes the full length of the affirmation of Christian faith, although Wieman comes nearer doing so than the other three. None of them, for example, moves into that dimension of Christian faith that affirms that man owes his ultimate origin to the creative word of the living God, in relation to whom man exists as responsible creature to Sovereign Creator. Yet this

[28]*See* Stewart G. Cole, *The History of Fundamentalism* (New York, 1931).

affirmation is basic in the perspective of Christian nurture. The significance of this affirmation will become more evident as we now consider some of the basic concepts and postulates of a Christian doctrine of man.

2. *The Christian Ground of Human Value*

ONE of these fundamental concepts is the idea of the worth of persons. Liberal culture, including liberal religion, has always professed reverence for human personality. Yet it is a paradoxical fact that liberal culture has involved reverence for man on the one hand and the devaluation of man on the other. Is there any explanation of this situation? It is never safe to generalize when dealing with a situation so complex as this; for all explanations are apt to seem themselves to be in need of explanation. There are, however, at least two factors that are involved in the tendency of modern culture to devalue man. One of these factors is practical, and is more or less inherent in the growth of industrial technology. The other lies in the realm of moral and religious theory.

Modern industrialism involves processes and technics that inherently tend toward a certain amount of dehumanization, and thus in effect toward devaluation of personality. Take, for example, the technological pattern and process of the textile industry. A few years ago, the President of the Cotton Textile Institute undertook to justify the current practice of the "stretch-out" on the ground that the textile weaver is not really a worker in the ordinary meaning of that term. "A weaver," he contended, "does not weave; a spinner does not spin. These functions are performed respectively by the looms and by the spinning frames. What these workers do mainly is to mend broken threads."[1] Just so! Yet if textile

[1] *The New York Times,* September 30, 1934, VIII, 2:7.

weaving does actually reduce the behavior of the operator to the routine work of mere thread-mending, how can it fail to produce more or less truncated personalities? What is true of textile technics is, in principle, true of many other highly developed types of mass industry. In such industries the center of creativity is located, not in man, but in the machine. The almost inevitable tendency is to obstruct the growth of human personality. It is true that many of these dehumanizing technics can, and should, be abolished. It is also true that shorter hours and other readjustments would greatly ameliorate the lot of the technological laborer. Yet when every conceivable improvement has been made, the modern machine-process will always be the means of a certain amount of dehumanization. That this has been a factor in the modern devaluation of man can hardly be denied.

There is, however, another factor in the contemporary tendency to devalue human personality; and it is with this factor that we are most concerned here. It lies in the realm of modern educational and religious thought, and is closely connected with what we in the foregoing section defined as naturalistic liberalism. It is true, of course, that naturalistic liberals have always made the principle of the worth of persons central in their theory. It thus seems contradictory to connect their thought with the current tendency to devalue man. Let it be admitted at once that these thinkers have not intended to espouse a theory which would devalue human personality; on the contrary, they have thought of themselves as laying the only foundations on which man could be truly valued. Nevertheless, it is a paradoxical fact that while naturalism professes respect for human value, it at the same time supports a theory of human worth which, from the point of view of Christian faith, cuts the ultimate root of the value of personality.

The central issue here was sharply raised by Julian Huxley in a recent article entitled, "Life Can Be Worth Living."[2] In this essay, Huxley, like naturalists in general, takes the position that man is the product of purely natural forces, and that in consequence human life is the source and center of its own worth. He admits, however, that man must be sustained by a faith of some sort, yet he himself can only say, "My final belief is in life." He becomes romantic in his affirmation of the dignity and the worth of man, and yet he vigorously denies that man is of worth beyond himself and his kind. Here, then, is a clear instance of what may be called a naturalistic or secular theory of human value, and of the problem it poses.

Against this theory, the Christian doctrine of human value becomes distinctive. The crucial difference lies in the fact that, for Christian faith, man is not a creature of purely secular or natural forces; he owes his creation ultimately to the living God. The ultimate root of the Christian worth of persons is therefore theocentric. Man's value, in other words, is derived, not autonomous; it inheres in the fact that man emerged out of divine love and lives only because of the nurturing love of his divine Creator. In three important respects, therefore, the theory of value underlying Christian nurture conflicts with secular theories of human value.

(*a*) In the first place, Christian nurture holds that human value is enhanced when it is connected with a transcendent source in God. On the other hand, secular humanists contend that human values undergo depreciation when they are identified in their origin and significance with a transcendent divine Being. Thus Dewey, in his *A Common Faith*, writes:

[2]"Living Philosophies, III," *The Nation,* CXLVII (1938), pp. 349–352. (Later collected and published in book form under title, *Living Philosophies: a Symposium.*)

"The contention of an increasing number of persons is that depreciation of natural social values has resulted, both in principle and in actual fact, from reference of their origin and significance to supernatural powers."[3]

This is a direct challenge to the Christian theory of human value, and one that cannot be ignored. If it be true that the reference of human values to a theocentric source has actually resulted in the depreciation of those values, then every religious educator should know this. But one should not accept Dewey's reading of the situation uncritically. Human experience gives an answer that is more complex than Dewey's statement seems to admit. While it doubtless is true that certain ideas of God have had the effect, in some instances, of debasing human value, it is none the less true that other ideas—specifically those embodied in the teachings of the eighth-century Prophets and Jesus—have resulted in the enhancement of human personality. When, furthermore, Dewey implies that devaluation of human social values must necessarily follow from their identification with any view of God as transcendent Being, he expresses a value-judgment that derives from what appears to be a prejudiced outlook. Dewey here reflects not only his antitheistic bias, but he reaches a verdict that he himself cannot sustain in terms of his own empirical method.[4]

[3] P. 71.

[4] In a recent work, *Liberalism and Social Action* (New York, 1935), Dewey seems to modify somewhat his earlier position. Reviewing the history of liberalism's quest for human values, he writes: "No account of the rise of humanitarian sentiment as a force in creation of the new regulations of industry would be adequate that did not include the names of religious leaders drawn from both dissenters and the Established Church. Such names as Wilberforce, Clarkson, Zachary, Macaulay, Elizabeth Fry, Hannah More, as well as Lord Shaftesbury, come to mind." P. 20 f.

Dewey contends in his *A Common Faith* that human values would at once be widely cherished and enhanced if only they were disconnected from their ground in a divine Being. This is typical of secular humanists. The assumption is that belief in an ultimate Valuer of human life is the main source of man's devaluation. Thus in secular circles it is often contended that the chief enemy of democracy inheres in the belief in a transcendent God. Abolish faith in God, it is said, and the main root of human tyranny will be cut. Political and cultural trends since the first World War should dispel this illusion. The new political faiths which today most explicitly reject the idea of God in the Christian sense are precisely those that are most militant in their affirmation of social and political dictatorship. How do human values fare under these new secular faiths? Christendom at its worst never perpetrated more inhumanity to man than is in practice among the secular popes of totalitarianism.

There is thus little evidence in contemporary events to support the claim that human values will be liberated and enriched if only they are dissociated from their source in God. On the other hand, it seems clear that the sure way to undermine the worth of human values is to deny their ultimate ground and valuation in God. "If you want to save social impulse," says William E. Hocking, "save the worth of men; and if you want to save the worth of men, find the worth of the cosmos in which man breathes and thinks."[5] In this penetrating statement, Hocking clearly confirms the Christian conception of the ultimate basis of human value.

(*b*) At a second and closely related point there is divergence between the Christian idea of the value of persons and

[5]"Does Civilization *Still* Need Religion?" *Christendom*, 1 (1935), p. 39.

that of naturalistic humanism. For the latter, humanity is the unit of supreme value. Beyond man there are no values with which culture should concern itself. Man's chief end therefore is to enrich life as its own ultimate good and highest value. There is, of course, no cosmic guarantee of human values.[6] Man must "accept the stern condition of being physically alone" in the universe.[7] Nevertheless, it is contended that this very cosmic isolation should inspire man to invest his life with enduring worth and dignity.

For Christian faith, on the other hand, humanity is not the unit of supreme value. Only God is supremely worthful. Man is, of course, a reality of high value, but his value is not wholly intrinsic or autonomous. It grows out of man's creaturely relation to God, and loses its Christian meaning when its connection with its divine source is denied or obscured. It follows from this that the Christian conception of human value makes man no mere end in himself. Human good, in fact, finds its true fulfilment only when it is committed to God as the supremely good. For Christian faith, man's highest end must always be the glorification of God. "Thou shalt worship the Lord thy God, and Him only shalt thou serve." It is said that the Puritans of early New England sometimes asked their prospective pastors the question, "Are you willing to be damned for the glory of God?" If at the root of this query there was an erroneous assumption, it yet emphasized the truth that it is possible so to glorify self or even society as to deny God as man's last end. Of this truth our contemporary world furnishes numerous examples.

[6]*Cf.* Arthur H. Dakin, *Man the Measure* (Princeton, 1939), p. 53. *See also* Edwin A. Burtt, *Types of Religious Philosophy* (New York, 1939), p. 366.
[7]M. C. Otto, *Things and Ideals* (New York, 1924), p. 290.

But, one may ask, does not the fulfilment of human life involve also the realization of God as the highest value? The answer, of course, is yes; but not without an important qualification. The fulfilment of human life, from the standpoint of Christian faith, is a paradoxical process. This paradoxical process lies at the heart of the Christian ethic. "For whosoever would save his life shall lose it; and whosoever shall lose his life for my sake and the gospel's shall save it."[8] This involves not merely that one should participate in the life of his fellows. It requires something more than that one should love his neighbor as himself, for the end of life involves more than human community. All of this may take place under a secular theory of human life; as may be seen, for example, in Marxian anthropology. The something more that is needed lies in the fact that man's true meaning is never realized in terms of purely human community, but only in terms of a reality that is the creative ground of all life and all community. He who does not commit himself to the glory of God as his chief good will always be tempted to endow relative values with a finality which they do not possess.

(c) This leads to a third respect in which the Christian idea of the value of persons is fundamentally different from that of secular humanism. As a child of God, and therefore as bearer of the divine image, man is worthful, according to Christian faith, not merely before his fellow men but also before God. In this view man's worth is never determined finally by the social estimate of human worth. No matter what society may conclude concerning the worth of human

[8]Mark 8:35. Unless indicated otherwise, all quotations from the Bible are taken from the American Revised Version, by permission of the International Council of Religious Education, holders of the copyright.

personality, man yet remains an object of precious worth to God. If man's worth were measurable in purely social scales, then the value of persons would fluctuate with the changing norms of social judgment. The value of man in that case might be measured at one time in terms of class, at another in terms of race, and at yet another in terms of nation. But Christian faith denies that human value ever can be measured in terms of the standards of human culture. Man remains "of more value than a sheep" regardless of whether mankind agrees or disagrees.

3. *The Root of Christian Individuality and Community*

CLOSELY RELATED to the question of the basis of human value is that of the transcendent root of individuality and community. Technological patterns of modern life have brought into the foreground of religious thought the problem of both individuality and human fellowship. The social emphasis in American Christianity and in religious education has run parallel with the growing consciousness of human interdependence. Along with this growth of social consciousness, however, certain modes of religious thought have emerged that have tended to obscure the Christian basis and meaning of individual selfhood on the one hand and of human community on the other. To the extent that this has happened, Christian nurture has been weakened at its root.

(*a*) *Individuality*. One aspect of this tendency has revealed itself in an extreme emphasis upon the social idea of the human self. Modern religious and educational thought has sought to correct the one-sided emphasis of older individualism. With the aid of modern psychology and sociology, the religious educator of the social-gospel mode of thought has stressed the social nature of human existence. Self and society, it is held, are conjunct and are implicated in each other. "Research has shown," says Coe, "that personal life, *qua* personal, is interpersonal."[1] This mode of thought has been a definite factor in the growth of the social theory of religious nurture. Under its influence the one-sidedness of older Protestant individualism was corrected.

Meanwhile, however, the consciousness of the unique character of the individual self has undergone decline.[2] This is partly due to the fact that recent thought has preoccupied itself with the idea of the social content of personality. While leaders in the social theory of religious education have by no means excluded the individual aspect of selfhood, nevertheless they have placed primary emphasis on the social aspect of the self. Thus while correcting a one-sided individualistic view of selfhood, they have tended toward an equally one-sided socialized view. But there is another reason—and a more important one—why this awareness of the unique individuality of the human self is on the decline. It derives from the fading sense of the divine source of human individuality.

It is at this point that the Christian view of man contains a most significant emphasis. In an earlier section of this chapter it was shown that Christianity holds that human existence derives ultimately from God. Implied in this fact is a truth that must be emphasized in this connection. For Christian faith not only regards humanity as a whole as

[1]"Religion, Education, Democracy," *Religious Education,* xxxv (1940), p. 132.
[2]For a penetrating analysis of the process by which modern culture dissipated the Christian idea of the individual, *see* Reinhold Niebuhr, *The Nature and Destiny of Man,* Vol. 1: *Human Nature* (New York, 1941), pp. 61–92.

deriving ultimately from God, but it sees each individual being as emerging by reason of a unique creative act of God. "Thou didst fashion *me* in my mother's womb."[3] Man's ultimate individuality is therefore inherent in the fact that he was called into being by a personal word of the living God.

Implicit in this idea of the theocentric root of individuality are two truths that are fundamental to the doctrine of Christian nurture. One of these relates to the idea of divine providence. From the fact that each individual self emerges in response to a creative act on the part of God, it follows that each self is the object of God's personal concern. From the point of view of human reason this, of course, seems impossible. "What is man that thou shouldst think of him? And the son of man that thou shouldst care for him?"[4] Nevertheless, this is a basic element of the Christian gospel. In such parables as the Lost Coin, the Lost Sheep, and the Lost Boy, Jesus clearly teaches God's unvarying concern for the individual.[5] There is joy in heaven over the *one* sinner who repents. This individualistic note runs throughout the gospels.

This emphasis is of primary importance in a time when the patterns of culture make it extremely difficult to consider man in terms of his own individual worth and destiny. When human existence is threatened with chaos, as at present, individuals will be tempted to seek to save themselves through lapsing into herd-men.[6] The merging of individual selves into great collectives of one sort or another is a marked trend of the times. In these circumstances, the idea that God

[3]Ps. 139:13.   [4]Ps. 8:4.   [5]Luke 15:1-32.
[6]Thus E. E. Aubrey says: "How to be socialized yet not be a victim to the group—this is the individual's dilemma." *Man's Search for Himself,* p. 159.

concerns Himself with the value of the individual will seem almost absurd. Men will tend to measure their value in terms of group value. In order to conserve their own worth they will exalt the worth of the group rather than of the individual. The present world crisis is everywhere accelerating this tendency.

There is a second and correlative truth that is inherent in the idea of the theocentric source of the self. As it implies that God exercises direct concern for each human self, so it implies that each self is dependent upon and responsible ultimately to God alone. In this idea of final responsibility to God alone lies the ultimate source of Christianity's radical individualism. No purely naturalistic doctrine of man can furnish the self with the basis necessary for prophetic individual insight and action. As already indicated, the naturalist regards the self as "created through the contacts of life."[7] In this view the self contains no metaphysical root, no ultimate basis for individuality. The self is the subjective aspect of social process, and therefore has no transcendental basis for radical social criticism and social rebellion.

On the other hand, the Christian orientation of individuality affords a basis for radical self-consciousness and prophetic self-direction. The self, from this point of view, derives its ultimate individuality from the fact of its unique relation to God. The "I" of the human person emerges only in virtue of a creator and sustainer "Thou."[8] The inner depth of the "I" cannot be fully apprehended on the plane of the purely social relations of the self. Nor can the inner experience of the "I" in relation to the "Thou" be fully expressed on the social plane. Reinhold Niebuhr is thus quite right

[7]M. C. Otto, *Things and Ideals,* p. 151.
[8]*Cf.* Emil Brunner, *Man in Revolt,* pp. 23–24.

when he says, "There are depths of consciousness in each individual self-consciousness which can never be completely exhausted in any social expression."[9] The full depth of the "I" can be experienced only in terms of the self's solitary confrontation of its "Creator-Thou." In this sense there is an important element of truth in Whitehead's claim that religion implicates the soul on its solitary plane of existence.[10] "The great religious conceptions which haunt the imaginations of civilized mankind," says Whitehead, "are scenes of solitariness: Prometheus chained to his rock, Mahomet brooding in the desert, the meditations of the Buddha, the solitary Man on the Cross."[11] In support of this general point of view, William E. Hocking recently wrote: "On the whole, the Founder of Christianity dwelt on the atomic aspect of the soul, in his emphasis on individual responsibility, and on the subordinate value of family ties, symbolized by the demand for rebirth. A man's ultimate relations are solely to God; and perhaps the deepest thing in Christianity is the adequacy with which it presents this ultimate solitude of the soul, not alone in birth, and in death, but in the history of its own ethical problem, which no man can meet for it."[12]

On the level of the solitary self, the Christian consciousness may apprehend values that are supra-social, and thus bring to bear upon both the self and society a revolutionary type of criticism. It is from this perspective that the Christian self-consciousness knows that "there is no one good." It is from

[9]*Reflections on the End of an Era* (New York, 1934), p. 92. *Cf.* E. E. Aubrey, *Man's Search for Himself*, p. 52.
[10]*Religion in the Making* (New York, 1926), pp. 16 f.
[11]*Ibid.*, pp. 19 f.
[12]*The Lasting Elements of Individualism* (New Haven, 1937), p. 22.

this perspective that Isaiah confesses: "Woe is me! for I am undone; because I am a man of unclean lips, and I dwell in the midst of a people of unclean lips."[13] This perspective issues not only in criticism of self and society, but it prompts the individual self to radical commitment. Thus Isaiah's vision found its logical outcome in his self-commitment: "Here am I; send me."[14] This self-commitment takes on its highest ethical significance only when it is realized that Isaiah committed himself to preach, not smooth platitudes, but a six-fold woe.[15] A perspective from the absolute ethic of the King-dom of God always brings conflict with conventional moral-ity. On the other hand, only the self that is made to confront that absolute ethic is apt persistently to challenge the existing moral and social situation.

(b) *Community*. Thus far we have attempted to show that true individuality must be understood from the theo-centric perspective of Christian faith. We may now affirm that this is also the perspective from which to understand the nature and dynamic of enduring community.

I take it that no one will question the desirability of a community of persons. In any event, the chaos of present existence leaves mankind no other reasonable alternative. Community of some sort we must have; the only question concerns what kind it shall be. At this point, however, a basic issue emerges. For two essentially divergent concepts of community bid for human allegiance in our time. One of these is a secular idea of community, based on a natural-istic understanding of man. This idea of community is demonstrated conspicuously in Marxism and the National Socialism of Nazi Germany. But it is by no means confined to Marxism and Nazism. The logic of the thought of such

[13]Isa. 6:5.   [14]Isa. 6:8.   [15]Isa. 5:8–24.

men as Dewey leads also to a naturalistic or secular doctrine of social community.[16] From this point of view the bond of community inheres in the social nature of human personality, and the dynamic of community arises out of love of man for man.

The other is the Christian concept of community. Christianity sees a more ultimate root of human community than secularism can offer. It believes with secularism that there are important bonds of community in the social nature of persons. Within the empirical context of human existence there are vital resources for the achievement of a large degree of fellowship. Nevertheless, the Christian frame of man provides a more ultimate ground of interdependence. Christian faith claims that all persons are children of one family in God. The ultimate bond of Christian community is therefore supra-social.

As Christian community contains a supra-social bond, so it also contains a dynamic that involves something more than interhuman love. The love that sustains Christian fellowship involves more than that which is presupposed by secular interpretations of community. The love that is embodied in the latter is a love that is nourished on interhuman resources. It is socially self-motivating. The ultimate meaning of its love is exhausted in the love of man for man. Its love-ethic is solely a social ethic. Love that moves on the Christian level is markedly unlike this. Its basic difference lies in the fact that it is theocentric. The love of the Christian springs out of the awareness of God's love as expressed, for example, in His acts of Creation and Redemption. Inasmuch

[16]*Cf.* Robert L. Calhoun, "The Dilemma of Humanitarian Modernism," *The Christian Understanding of Man* (An Oxford Conference Book), pp. 57–68.

as "God so loved the world," the Christian man is drawn
to Him in the love of creature for Creator.

The love of the Christian is theocentric in yet another
sense. In the Christian concept of community, God is the
supreme object of man's love. It is true that the twofold
commandment of Jesus includes both love to God and love
to man. But it is important to note that love to God is to be
with "all thy heart, soul, mind, and strength," and love to
neighbor only "as thyself." Does any one claim that he should
love himself as much as he should love God? It is true that
the Bible says, "He that sayeth I love God, and hateth his
brother, is a liar." Also, it says that "inasmuch as ye have
done it unto one of the least of these, ye have done it unto
me." There is nothing in these or similar statements, however, to lead one to suppose that man should love another
person or even humanity as a whole as much as he should
love God.

4. Image of God and Sinner

THE CHRISTIAN perspective of human life involves a realistic
understanding of the nature of man. The nature of human
nature is a problem which has greatly concerned the modern
religious educator. Under the influence of psychology and
sociology, numerous articles and books have been written on
this question during the past generation. That the researches
of these sciences have enriched our insight into human nature at certain important points cannot be denied.[1] They
have, for example, revealed that human nature is, within
limits, modifiable; that there are marked individual differ-

[1] For a valuable brief summary of the contributions of psychology
to an understanding of human nature, *see* Harrison S. Elliott, *Bearing
of Psychology upon Religion,* Chap. 1.

ences between persons; and that human personality contains within itself important resources for religious growth.

At the same time it must be admitted that these psychological studies have not given the Christian educator a sufficiently realistic insight into the contradictory character of human existence. To be sure, religious educators have admitted that human nature is to some extent the scene of inner conflict. Nevertheless, left-wing liberals, as a rule, have regarded these inner tensions as a more or less passing phase of moral and cultural evolution. In other words, they are "due to the atavistic pull of inherited but outgrown goods."[2] It has been assumed, moreover, that the egoistic impulses are less tenacious than the altruistic ones, and that in the long run selfishness is doomed to defeat itself.[3] If we consider society in its historical perspective, says George A. Coe, "we perceive that it is, on the whole, an evolutionary process in which we are working out the beast, and training ourselves to have regard for what is humane."[4] It is obvious that on these terms man's contradictory existence cannot be taken very seriously. In particular, man as sinner cannot be regarded as an object of fundamental Christian concern.

Indeed, it is a significant fact that progressive religious educators have usually sought to avoid the use of the term sin in their description of the nature of man.[5] "Most re-

[2]Mathews, "Theology as Group Belief" in *Contemporary American Theology,* ed. Vergilius Ferm (New York, 1933), p. 186.

[3]Coe, *A Social Theory of Religious Education,* p. 168.

[4]*Ibid.,* p. 167.

[5]Many of the more influential books in liberal theory of religious education do not even list the term sin as a primary heading in their indices. *See,* for example, E. S. Ames, *Psychology of Religious Experience;* Bower, *The Curriculum of Religious Education; Religion and the Good Life;* Hugh Hartshorne, *Childhood and Character* (Boston, 1919); *Character in Human Relations* (New York, 1932). A notable

ligious educators," says Stewart G. Cole, "can discuss intelligently the subject of man without any expressed need" for the term sin.[6] Many religious educators thus seem to agree with Harry Elmer Barnes that "sin is an anachronism and a confusing superstition."[7] They admit, of course, that human nature is a complex of tendencies, some of which impel the person in one direction and some in another. This situation, however, is not considered to be illuminated by the use of the term sin. Thus George H. Betts gave psychology the chief credit for discarding from the religious educator's vocabulary the term sin, and especially the term original sin.[8]

This change in terminology represents something more fundamental than the mere abandonment of an old term. That modern culture is marked by a fading sense of sin has long been admitted by liberals.[9] Concomitant with the fading consciousness of sin has been the growing consciousness of the natural goodness of human nature. That this was the trend of American religious thought during the nineteenth century was made clear in Chapter One of this work. With the emergence of the twentieth-century movement in religious education this trend was continued and even ac-

---

exception is Coe's *A Social Theory of Religious Education,* which devotes an entire chapter to the subject of sin. *See also* Harrison Elliott's recent book, *Can Religious Education Be Christian?* Chap. VIII.

[6]"Where Religious Education and Theology Meet," *Religious Education,* xxxv (1940), p. 21.

[7]*The Twilight of Christianity* (New York, 1929), p. 209. *See also* p. 283.

[8]"Let Religious Education Beware," *Christian Century,* XLIV (1927), p. 496.

[9]At the opening of the twentieth century Coe wrote: "The sense of sin is certainly not present as it once was." *The Religion of a Mature Mind,* p. 369. In his *Normative Psychology of Religion,* p. 147, Wieman has more recently spoken of the fading sense of sin.

celerated. The educational theory of the liberal Church is still largely in the grip of a romantic doctrine of man, despite the changes that have taken place in American life and thought since the first World War. The liberal religious educator's doctrine of man is unrealistic in three basic respects.

(*a*) It is unrealistic in its one-sided interpretation of the doctrine of the *Imago Dei*. The ruling emphasis given to this doctrine in modern Protestant nurture was revealed by William H. P. Faunce in an address before the Religious Education Association in 1904. "The center of studies is for us," he said, "the nature of the child, made in the image of God, and revealing God at every stage of its growth."[10] From the context it is clear that Faunce was concerned to stress the idea of the essential divinity of human nature as reflected in the child. From the fact that man was created in the image of God, he arrives at the position that human nature is naturally good. A similar conclusion was expressed by Washington Gladden a decade later: "If God is the Father of us all . . . there can be no contrariety between our nature and his."[11] In this same general trend of thought Coe says, "To Tertullian's argument that the soul is naturally Christian we may now add that the child is naturally Christian."[12]

This interpretation of the *Imago Dei* obscures, and in effect often denies, the contradiction[13] between man in his original creation and man in his present empirical existence. Thus it destroys the Christian basis on which man may be viewed

[10]*Proceedings of the Second Annual Convention of the Religious Education Association* (Philadelphia, 1904), p. 77.

[11]*Present Day Theology* (Columbus, Ohio, 1913), p. 138.

[12]*A Social Theory of Religious Education*, p. 145.

[13]On the nature and source of man's contradictory existence, *see* Emil Brunner's illuminating study, *Man in Revolt* (Eng. tr., New York, 1939), Chaps. VI–VII.

as both in the image of God and as sinner. It is the Christian faith that man in his original existence was so created in the divine image as to be in full fellowship with God, and therefore as being without the consciousness of sin. But this faith also holds that man lost this original consciousness of the divine communion through disobedience, and thus became aware of himself as sinner. In man's disobedience the divine image becomes perverted, although not to the extent that man loses all consciousness of himself as child of God. Thus in one and the same act of Christian self-consciousness man is aware of himself as both child of God and sinner.

It is the weakness of a liberal theory of human nature, however, that it has emphasized the godlikeness of the human creature to the neglect of his sinfulness. It is possible, of course, to reverse this emphasis, as was demonstrated in Protestant orthodoxy against which Channing and Bushnell revolted in the nineteenth century. Orthodoxy had committed itself to a doctrine of total depravity, and had thereby lost the consciousness of man's godlikeness as implicated in the divine image. It failed to recognize that, even from the psychological viewpoint, man's consciousness of himself as sinner involves at one and the same time consciousness of himself as child of God, and therefore as being something more than sinner. The transcendental act by which man judges himself to be sinner is possible only because man knows himself to be a child of God. A paradoxical view of human existence may be lost either by an overemphasis upon human goodness or upon human depravity. If orthodoxy lost this paradoxical idea through the latter tendency, liberalism has lost it through the former. A realistic understanding of human nature requires man to see himself as both child of God and sinner, and not merely as one or the other.

(*b*) A second aspect of unrealism in liberal theory of human nature lies in its one-sided emphasis upon the source of sin in what Walter Rauschenbusch called "the super-personal forces" of society. This trend is the outgrowth of many factors, two of which are primary. In the first place, and basically, it is the response of the Church to the new forms of collective evil that sprang up with modern urban-industrial civilization. In the second place, it is the response of the Church to the growth of the psycho-sociological emphasis upon the idea that "beyond the feeble and short-lived individual towers the social group as a super-personal entity."[14] Thus the Church shifted its major attention from the source of sin in the self to the source of sin in the social group. Coe recently charted his own earlier intellectual growth in these words: "Beginning with the early nineties, if not before, my notions of good and evil were shifting towards social relations and the social order."[15]

This shift in emphasis served as a necessary corrective of the one-sided individualism of orthodoxy. At a time when evangelical orthodoxy was preoccupied with petty sins of the atomic individual, the social-gospel movement forced the Church to recognize that gigantic forms of social evil spring out of groups possessing great economic and technological power. This insight must be preserved in any theory of Christian nurture that hopes to deal realistically with human existence in the modern world.[16]

At the same time it must be recognized that Christian

[14]Rauschenbusch, *A Theology for the Social Gospel*, p. 110.

[15]"My Own Little Theatre," in *Religion in Transition*, p. 110.

[16]For demonstration of this truth *see* John C. Bennett's penetrating essay, "The Causes of Social Evil," in *Christian Faith and the Common Life*. (Vol. IV: Official Oxford Conference Book, 1938), pp. 175–195.

faith does not find the ultimate source of sin and evil in super-personal groups or social systems, but rather in the private order of the human self. Christian faith knows that "The heart is deceitful above all things, and it is exceedingly corrupt: who can know it?"[17] Christian faith does not permit man to indulge the romantic hope that when a particular social system, such as capitalism, slavery, or militarism, is destroyed, the root of evil will be eradicated. On the contrary, when a particular system of evil is uprooted, the human self is only freed for new forms of evil.[18] It is good and necessary to abolish particular patterns of evil, yet Christian realism is never under the illusion that this will destroy the root of evil in the human self. When liberalism gave itself over to the idea that man is naturally good, it easily succumbed to the illusion that the root of sin ultimately resides in "super-personal" forces.

(c) Liberal theory of human nature is also unrealistic in its tendency to interpret sin primarily in terms of interhuman relations. The theocentric aspect of sin has been not so much denied as minimized or obscured. "When I was a boy," says Coe, "I was taught that sin is a relation, not between me and my neighbor, but between me and God. Subsequent reflection has led me to regard the distinction here made as not valid. . . . The dwelling place of the Highest is not apart from, but within, the brotherhood, which is the family of God and the kingdom of God."[19]

Coe's emphasis here is the logical outgrowth of his theory of divine immanence. It represents a real gain insofar as it

[17]Jer. 17:9.
[18]For example, the Civil War uprooted evil in the form of chattel slavery, but it took new root in the system of share-cropping that replaced slavery.
[19]*A Social Theory of Religious Education,* p. 164.

shows that sinful conduct has its social context, and that sin is never a purely private transaction between the sinner and God. It cannot be denied that pietistic orthodoxy was sorely in need of the liberal's criticism at this point. But on the other hand it cannot be denied that the social theory of religious education has had a tendency in many circles to obscure the theocentric side of sin and to place an overemphasis upon sin as antisocial conduct. In a review of religious thought for the first quarter of the twentieth century, Gerald Birney Smith wrote: "The conception of sin has been profoundly affected by the modern interest in social problems, and *is rapidly losing its metaphysical content.*"[20]

Against this general tendency, Christianity protests. For it is the Christian faith that human sin is directed ultimately against God, the ground of human existence and the source of human salvation. In this sense, therefore, human sin is ultimately a revolt against God alone. David caught a glimpse of the final import of sin when, in his anguish of soul over having had Uriah slain, he said, "I have sinned against Jehovah."[21] David, to be sure, was not unaware of the fact that he had sinned also against Uriah. Nevertheless, he rightly recognized that the ultimate tragedy of his sin lay in his revolt against God, the source of Uriah, Bathsheba, and all human existence. A great psalmist later expressed this central truth even more forcefully:

> Against thee, thee only, have I sinned,
> And done that which is evil in thy sight.[22]

This basic truth is set forth also by Jesus in the parable of the Final Judgment. "Inasmuch as ye did it unto one of

[20]*Religious Thought in the Last Quarter Century* (Chicago, 1927), p. 107. Italics added.
[21]2 Sam. 12:13.   [22]Ps. 51:4.

these my brethren, even these least, ye did it unto me."[23]
The element usually emphasized in this parable is humanitarian service. Thus the stress is placed upon what men do
for or against one another with only secondary attention to
the divine aspect. But in reality the Biblical emphasis is on
the divine aspect. The ethical focus for Jesus is God. It should
be noted that this parable includes both the positive and
the negative aspects of human conduct. It thus signifies that
in every act, whether expressive of loyalty or disloyalty, the
ultimate reality involved in human conduct is God.

It is only as human sinfulness is viewed from a theocentric perspective that it assumes its most tragic meaning from
the point of view of Christian faith. Thus the term sin is
necessarily a theological category. Those religious educators
who renounce a theocentric interpretation of the human situation are therefore quite right in discarding the term sin.
They rightly look to the empirical sciences for a more appropriate term. They are quite right also in declining to view
human sinfulness in its tragic dimensions. For sin becomes
really tragic only to those who interpret it from the divine
perspective.

[23]Matt. 25:40.

CHAPTER FOUR

FAITH IN THE DIVINE INITIATIVE

TWO MAJOR PURPOSES have directed our thought in the last two chapters. An effort was made to show, first, why the social-gospel concept of the Kingdom is in need of revision, and, second, wherein the doctrine of man as reflected in liberal Protestant nurture is defective. On this background let us next consider the question: What is the Christian understanding of the gospel?

1. Decadent Evangelism

THE CURRENT effort to re-examine the nature of the Christian gospel is in itself a tacit confession that the evangelical resources of Protestantism are less than adequate to cope with the present problems of personal and social life. Indeed, this is often openly acknowledged. Many Christian leaders find themselves in substantial agreement with the verdict of Richard Niebuhr: "The church has seen all mankind involved in crisis and has sought to offer help—only to discover the utter insufficiency of its resources."[1]

The problem of a vital evangelism should be of special interest to the twentieth-century Christian educator. For liberal Protestant nurture began with Bushnell's effort to combat a sterile form of revivalistic evangelism. During the

[1] H. Richard Niebuhr, W. Pauck, and F. P. Miller, *The Church Against the World* (Chicago, 1935), p. 5.

past generation his doctrine of evangelism through Christian nurture has been widely disseminated. Liberal Protestant educators have believed that Christian nurture would be the means of quickening the evangelical life of the American churches. Their faith involved two aspects. First, they believed in the revitalizing power of the child-centered Church.[2] To the question, "What must the church do to be saved?" the most typical answer of the religious educator during the 1920's was, "Build its program around childhood."[3] Second, they believed in the evangelical potency of the educational method. The traditional mode of revivalistic evangelism was rejected, except as a secondary method of converting those remaining adults who had not already responded to the process of educational evangelism during childhood.[4]

Like all American enterprises, this quest for an awakened Church through educational evangelism was pursued with energy and enthusiasm. Soon after the present century began, Coe expressed amazement "that salvation by education" had never received "doctrinal recognition."[5] In 1921, Betts urged that the "control of the church should gradually, but without unnecessary delay, be *taken over*" by the religious educator.[6] It is in this spirit that Protestantism carried out a crusade of educational evangelism during the past generation.

What have been the results from the standpoint of evan-

[2]*Cf.* Coe, *The Religion of a Mature Mind,* p. 326.
[3]For a set of popular posters expressing this viewpoint, *see* G. H. Betts, *The New Program of Religious Education* (New York, 1921), pp. 107 ff.
[4]*Ibid.,* p. 59.
[5]*The Religion of a Mature Mind,* pp. 249 ff.
[6]*The New Program of Religious Education,* p. 75. Italics added.

gelism? If by evangelism one means the institutional growth
of religion, then it cannot be denied that the educational
method has been, on the whole, reasonably successful. Statis-
tical studies show that present-day recruits of the Church are
coming largely through the church school and its allied agencies. But if by evangelism one refers not so much to numerical
growth as to a new dynamic in the Church which makes it
socially effective and world-redemptive, and which therefore sets the Christian community in radical tension with a
secular culture, then the answer is much less reassuring. That
institutional religion is implicated in the forces that are erod-
ing the Christian evangel is a fact that is admitted by those
within as well as those without the Church. To what extent
the Church would have been in even greater bondage
to a world-affirming spirit unless religious education had
emerged, we have no way of knowing.

The religious educator must, however, face two facts.
(1) In the first place, he must face the fact that the child-
centered Church does not in itself guarantee a quickened
religious faith. It merely assures the perpetuation of the
Church as an institution. It is true, of course, that no Church
can fail to retain its children and still preserve its institutional
existence. Yet the Church may even foster the child within
its fellowship and still not experience religious re-invigora-
tion. Indeed, the very numerical expansion of the Church
through the process of child-nurture may lead the Church
to assume that it is alive, when in reality it is dying at its
dynamic root. For, in fact, the easiest task of the Church is
to secure its formal existence through the nurture of childhood. As a very dependent creature, the child will naturally
tend to assimilate the mores of the adult life of the Church.
The Church should remember that great periods of reli-

gious rebirth have not emerged as the result of child-nurture. Religion has always come alive in the adult consciousness, and has usually involved a break with the religion inherited in childhood. The Christian Church, for example, had its birth in a new type of religious experience among those who revolted against conventional religion. So it has seemed to be ever since. Revolutionary waves of religious awakening come to a focus in a Saint Paul, a Saint Francis, a Luther, a Wesley, or an Edwards. Their experiences are then communicated to the young. But the insights and experiences of the awakeners tend to fade out in the experience of the second and third generations. Ideally, this should not be the case. For if the nurture of the young were sufficiently vital, religious values would presumably be retained and enriched in the succeeding generations. Such, however, has not seemed true in the past. On the contrary, the primary experiences of the prophets tend to become secondary experiences in their children, and especially in their children's children.[7] In the course of time a new innovation of a radical sort has to take place if the fires of religious vitality are to be rekindled.

The inference to be drawn from this fact is not that the Church should renounce the function of Christian nurture. On the contrary, to the fullest possible extent the Church should share its life and faith with the young. This is a basic and continuing task of the Church. Nevertheless, the Church must not surrender to the illusion that child-nurture, in itself, will rekindle the fire of life and faith in the Christian community. For the religion of the child will usually

[7] In *The Plain Man Seeks for God* (New York, 1933), pp. 20–24, Henry P. Van Dusen gives a vivid description of this tendency in American Protestantism during the past four generations.

be a relatively pale edition of the faith of the older generation. This means that unless the faith comes alive in the
soul of some mature individual or group religious vitality
may be expected to continue to decline in modern culture.

(2) Again, the fact must be faced that religious educators
have been much too optimistic in respect of the religious
potency of the educational method. In the first flush of
religious education not a few leaders could say, ". . . we
are now in the first stages of a great religious revival which
takes the direction of the Christian nurture of the young."[8]
Here is one of the early prophecies of what would take place
under the influence of the educational method:

> More sides of a man's nature will be touched at once, and the
> tendency to dramatic climaxes will be correspondingly lessened.
> Further, attention will be turned outward rather than inward, for
> the very essence of the social spirit of the Gospel is that each re-
> gards not his own things, but rather the things of others. Emo-
> tion there will be, but the social emotions will be prominent, and
> they are gentle and pervasive rather than explosive. Surgery and
> purgative medicines will be less· in evidence, but wholesome
> atmosphere and life in the sunlight of that love of God which
> includes the love of men, and of that love of men which includes
> the love of God, will be no less effective.[9]

For a full generation now this "wholesome atmosphere"
has been fostered in the liberal Protestant Churches. These
churches revolted against the excesses and imbecilities of
revivalism; they spurned catastrophic conversion; they condemned religious introversion and unhealthy emotionalism.
Well enough! For in truth the tragedy of traditional revivalism was that it no longer really revived. It had become
largely a psychological substitute for a dynamic awakening.

Nevertheless, the educational method has not brought in

[8]Coe, *The Religion of a Mature Mind,* p. 298.   [9]*Ibid.,* p. 289.

the revival of religion that the educators confidently promised. It has not been the religiously reconstructive force that was contemplated. Perhaps too much was expected of it. In any event, there is little hope that liberal nurture in its present form can keep religion prophetically alive in our culture. Why is this type of nurture so impotent? There is no simple answer to this question. There is, however, one sort of answer that seems worth serious exploration. It is this: Liberal Protestant nurture is feeble because it is rooted in a sub-Christian gospel. Educational evangelism is largely sterile, we contend, because, despite its protestations, it is without an adequate evangel. Wherein this seems true we shall undertake to show in the remainder of this chapter.

2. *Jesus Christ as the Ultimate Meaning of Life*

THE CHRISTIAN gospel involves a fundamental faith in respect to the relation of God to human history. An important aspect of that faith we have already discussed in our analysis of the Christian understanding of man. We saw, for example, that, according to the Christian perspective, man emerged in response to the Divine Initiative. We are now ready to take another step in Christian faith, and with it to extend our understanding of the doctrine of Christian nurture. This step involves the faith that God has revealed in history, in Jesus Christ, the ultimate meaning and destiny of human existence.

This statement has many aspects that might be pursued, but the point of emphasis here is that history was given a religious center in Jesus Christ, in the sense that historical events, both past and future, find their ultimate spiritual significance in and through Christ. The events B.C. and A.D.

are intersected by a transempirical "event" that discloses the ultimate religious meaning of historical existence before the end of the empirical time-process. In this sense therefore Christ is the center of history.[1] Thus for the Christian consciousness Christ is not a way, but The Way; not a truth but The Truth; not a life, but The Life.[2]

It is a well-known fact that the idea of revelation, in the classical sense, has not occupied a central place in modern theological thought. Indeed, J. M. Creed recently expressed the opinion that the Christian idea of revelation became entirely lost to liberal Protestant thought in the early part of the nineteenth century.[3] A shift from the traditional view of revelation was basically the result of the growth of modern science, notably the development of an evolutionary conception of life and culture, combined with the application of the method of higher criticism to the Bible.

By the time the twentieth-century movement of liberal nurture emerged the Christian idea of revelation had been greatly attenuated in American theology. Liberal nurture, it seems fair to say, has never greatly concerned itself with the idea of Christian revelation in the historic sense. Liberal religious educators, to be sure, have often referred to the fact that the divine element may be found in nature, and especially in human nature. They have also frequently advanced the idea that God continuously reveals himself.[4] But the idea of revelation in the sense that in Jesus Christ God disclosed

[1] *Cf.* Paul Tillich, "The Kingdom of God and History," in *The Kingdom of God and History* (Vol. III: Official Oxford Conference Books, Chicago, 1938), p. 119.

[2] John 4:16.

[3] *The Divinity of Jesus Christ, A Study in the History of Christian Doctrine since Kant* (Cambridge, 1938), pp. 12 ff. *Cf.* Chap. VI.

[4] *Cf.* Elliott, *Can Religious Education Be Christian?*, pp. 132–133.

the ultimate meaning of existence is quite foreign to the thought of most liberal educators, and especially to those who belong to the "progressive" wing of religious nurture.

Implicit in the philosophy of progressive nurture is the assumption that all "revelations" are relative, and that disclosure of the ultimate meaning of life necessarily must be reserved to some future moment in the history of mankind. Thus it finds itself in basic conflict with the Christian claim that God already has unveiled the meaning of existence before the end of the time-process. This conflict may be evaded or obscured by ambiguous statements, yet there is no denying the fact that it exists.

(a) The conflict is implicit, in the first place, in the progressive religious educator's constant and exaggerated emphasis on the importance of the present and the future. The past is not denied, to be sure, but it is placed in subordination to the present. Thus Bower recently stated in emphatic terms that it "is a naive illusion to suppose that ideas, values, . . . which functioned in a past period of culture, will or can function in the contemporary scene."[5]

Implicit in Bower's statement is a principle of relativism which, if logically and completely applied, would seem to make the insights of Jesus obsolete. The most one might say of Jesus, on this basis, is that his ideas and values are an historical exhibit of what modern Christians need not take seriously. The assumption, however, that historical ideas and values are entirely relative is in effect to deny that the message of Jesus can be normative in Christian nurture.

Thus Protestant nurture is confronted with the question

[5]"The Challenge of Reaction to Liberal Thought," *Religious Education,* XXXII (1937), p. 120. And yet, Bower is author of a stimulating book, in which he writes a whole chapter on "Recovering the Religious Values of the Bible"! See *The Living Bible,* Chap. XIV.

of old, "Art thou he that cometh, or look we for another?"[6]
The theory of progressive religious education is either obscure or negative in its answer to this question. In its one-
sided emphasis on the relativity of values it can hardly be
expected to give a positive answer. Nevertheless, the progressive is loath to accept the full consequences of such a position;
and therefore he continues to profess devotion to the ethical
teachings of Jesus, or at least to the spirit of quest as exhibited
in Jesus. Thus he is caught on the horns of a dilemma. To
admit an absolute revelation in Jesus would undermine his
relativistic principle; but to identify Jesus with an outmoded stage in revelation would weaken his devotion to
Jesus' ethical ideals. Confronted with this situation, the progressive vacillates from one side to the other. The result is
confusion and impotence where there should be clarity and
power.

(b) The tendency to deny that Jesus Christ is the revelation of life's ultimate meaning is implicit also in the educational method of progressive nurture. On the assumption
that reality is in process of continuous change, emphasis is
placed upon the method of experimental quest. The inference is, of course, that ultimate truth about human existence
is to emerge at some time in the distant future. Meanwhile,
therefore, one must seek the center of meaning not in values
that lie in the past, but in the quest for values that are to be
created in the present and in the future.

This experimentalist method is largely the fruit of pragmatic philosophy. The primary importance of method is
implicit in pragmatism.[7] As Dewey has reminded us, "there

[6]Matt. 11:3.
[7]Cf. John Dewey, et al., Creative Intelligence (New York, 1917),
pp. 55 ff.

are a steadily increasing number of persons who find security in methods of inquiry, of observation, experiment, of forming and following working hypotheses. Such persons are not unsettled by the upsetting of any special belief, because they retain security of procedure. They can say, borrowing language from another context, though this method slay my most cherished belief, yet will I trust it."[8] From this point of view it is natural that Dewey's first important treatise on educational philosophy should have concerned itself with how one thinks.[9]

The method of experimentalism, however, has been fostered by liberal religion as well as by modern pragmatic philosophy. Liberalism, it has been urged, is primarily a method of discovering truth, not any particular formulation of it.[10] Thus from the side of religious liberalism, as well as from the educational philosophy of Dewey, the movement in progressive Protestant nurture has been stimulated to concern itself chiefly with method.

In its anti-historical bias, progressive nurture has always been inclined to deny the value of content-teaching as such. It is not the purpose of Christian nurture, it is said, to teach the thought-products of the past, but rather to teach methods of inquiry, of experiment. By this approach, it is urged, traditionalism may be transcended and authoritarianism be

[8]Dewey, "Fundamentals," *The New Republic*, xxxvii (1924), p. 276.

[9]*How We Think* (New York, 1910).

[10]*Cf*. E. E. Aubrey, *Present Theological Tendencies*, pp. 25–29; Miles H. Krumbine, ed., *The Process of Religion* (New York, 1933), pp. 17–52; George Tyrrell, "The Prospects of Modernism," *Hibbert Journal*, vi (1907–8), p. 248; C. W. Emmet, "The Modernist Movement in the Church of England," *Journal of Religion*, ii (1922), pp. 561–576; F. H. Foster, *The Modern Movement in American Theology* (New York, 1939), p. 213.

repelled. The implication of this extreme emphasis on methodology is revealed in a forthright statement by Bower. "It is not the function of those upon whom the responsibility of religious leadership rests to *teach* the end-products of a past religious experience."[11]

Considered in itself, this statement suggests that Bower would have Christian nurture give no concern to historical values. Bower, however, does not go that far. Nevertheless, this is his way of strongly emphasizing the fact that the religious educator must focus the teaching process in present experience. For Bower, the chief significance of the Bible lies in the fact that it contains a long and complex record of a quest for truth, rather than in the fact that it discloses any ultimate truth.[12] Thus when he emphasizes the importance of "recovering the values of the Bible," what he means is that one should seek to recover the spirit of creative search which is demonstrated in the Bible. For, in a world of continuous change and evolutionary growth, the only sort of permanent value that can be conceived—and this Bower recognizes—is that of creative quest for the abundant life.

Thus progressive nurture, by reason of its underlying assumptions in respect of cultural evolution, is forced to adopt an experimental method which necessarily tends to underestimate the worth of historical values, including those of the Bible. The main concern is not with the recovery of any particular past religious insight, but with the process of remaking all insights. The important thing, therefore, is not the content of thought, but the technic of thought. Thus it is clear that the tendency of experimental method is to make little use of historical values except as a means of showing how people once carried on a search for truth. On this basis

[11]*The Living Bible*, p. 28.   [12]*Ibid.*, pp. 203–204.

the motive of Bible study would be reduced to a sort of antiquarian curiosity, and Jesus would become outmoded except perhaps as an ancient example of religious quest. If progressivism has not yet fully arrived at this point, it is only because it has not yet cleared itself of its pervasive ambiguity.

(c) The same general tendency is implicit also in the progressive educator's emphasis upon the principle of tentativeness. This principle, like the one discussed in the preceding section, is rooted in the presupposition that the world is in process of continuous change, and that therefore all values of previous historical existence are in process of being superseded. The ultimate light on life's meaning awaits some future unveiling in the time-process. Creative nurture is thus oriented in terms of that assumption, and it must accordingly reject or obscure the historic meaning of Christian revelation. The progressive religious educator will, of course, relate the past to the present in recognition of the continuity of experience, but he will do so only as a means of discovering "the growing point" in the present and the future.[13]

It is on this background that the idea of tentativeness as advocated by progressive educational theory must be understood. The world-process is in a state of continuous change; it is, as the empiricists say, an "open universe." Therefore ideas, postulates, and conclusions must be held, not as fixed, but as tentative and always subject to change. One overzealous convert to the principle of tentativeness even went so far as to say that the problem of whether or not an unchanging God exists will lose all importance if the educator

---

[13]*Cf.* Bower, "Points of Tension Between Progressive Religious Education and Current Theological Trends," in *Religious Education,* XXXIV (1939), pp. 167–169.

will only make up his mind not to fear change and to "rest in the fluidity of a world of continuous change."[14]

Occasionally we find the full implication of this principle made explicit in the theory of Protestant nurture. Few leaders in religious education have spoken more clearly in this respect than Sophia L. Fahs. In an address before the annual convention of the Religious Education Association in 1928, she said: "No longer can religious education be the simple process of instructing children in a way already decided upon as best; no longer can it be a passing on of moral principles even though in a most persuasive manner; . . . Religious growth and education in religion we must learn to conceive of as a process of questioning, of experimenting, in thought and in conduct."[15] How she would cultivate the tentative and the experimental temper is revealed in her attitude toward children's questions. "To us," she proceeds, "children's questions are opportunities not for us to give answers, but opportunities for stimulating children to further questionings."[16] This method is followed, she explains, in order to show children that they must seek to find their sense of security, not in answers to life's meaning, but "in the process of search."

The type of uncritical indoctrination against which Mrs. Fahs is seeking to safeguard children is clearly evident in the history of Protestant nurture. She knows, as does every informed person, that religious history affords many painful illustrations of dogmatic teaching. Any mode of nurture that fails to take account of the interests, capacities, and in-

[14]Blanche Carrier, *Church Education for Family Life* (New York, 1937), p. 73.

[15]"Changes Necessary in Elementary Religious Education Due to Conflicts Between Science and Religion," *Religious Education,* XXIII (1928), p. 333.

[16]*Ibid.,* p. 336.

dividual differences of children is, to be sure, subject to criticism. On the other hand, the teaching technic proposed by Mrs. Fahs is certainly not less objectionable. To think that the child can be religiously nourished by a series of interrogations is fatuous. Any such wily dodging of one question by asking the pupil another finally betrays itself into a form of vacillation, cowardice, or superficiality. It is dishonest for the teacher to pretend that he teaches pupils merely how to think, for the *how* always involves some kind of content or else all teaching is meaningless. Those who pose as mere guides as to how to think usually reveal at some point or other in the process rather clear-cut convictions, or else a pathetic vacuity of mind and insight.

The view that ideas should always be held in a wholly tentative fashion, is, from a psychological point of view, in need of critical reconsideration. J. H. Randall, Jr., has posed a crucial issue for religious educators in the form of three searching questions: "Can a man entertain all ideas as provisional hypotheses, subject to rigorous criticism and constant reconstruction, and at the same time cherish in feeling and action the conviction of the prophet and the saint of old? Can he vigorously crusade for a right he knows is relative and tentative? Can he pour out his soul in worship of a force or an ideal he knows may be superseded tomorrow?"[17]

Vital Christian nurture is rooted in a faith that cannot accept unqualifiedly this provisional temper and process of experimentalism. Christian nurture presupposes a faith that goes deeper than mere faith in "growing values." To be sure, the Christian educator will accept truly scientific fact, and he will not blindly assume that there is nothing new to be

[17]"The Rôle of Science in Modern Life: What Must Religion Learn From It?" *Religious Education,* xxv (1930), p. 114.

found in the human quest for truth. But also the Christian must not be blind to the fact that he lives finally by faith in a Christian revelation. The Christian teacher, therefore, does not share his faith in Christ with the child in a spirit of absolute tentativeness, but in the conviction that in Christ God has spoken an eternally valid word to humanity. A dynamic Christian Church has never taken seriously the idea that the gospel is to be preached and taught in a spirit of complete scientific objectivity. Indeed, the gospels are not themselves the result of that sort of objective teaching and preaching. "The first Christians," says Martin Dibelius, "had no interest in reporting the life and passion of Jesus objectively to mankind, *sine ira et studio*."[18]

In saying that the Christian educator should present Christ as the ultimate truth about human existence, there is no thought of implying that any particular interpretation of Jesus is itself the absolute truth. For, in the history of the Christian movement, what Jesus Christ has meant to human experience has been expressed in many different forms of thought. This process of changing thought-forms may be expected to continue if concepts are to be kept in vital relation to religious experience.[19] Nevertheless, changing formulations of the Christian revelation are not incompatible with the belief that Christ himself remains the ultimate meaning of human life.[20]

[18]*Gospel Criticism and Christology* (London, 1935), p. 16.

[19]In this connection, Archbishop Temple rightly says: "The revelation is not a doctrine or a system of theology or a code of ethics or a way of life; it is a Life actually lived, culminating in actual Death and actual Resurrection, upon the plane of history." *Revelation,* ed. John Baillie and Hugh Martin (New York, 1937), p. 104.

[20]For a brilliant exposition of this truth, *see* H. Richard Niebuhr, *The Meaning of Christian Revelation* (New York, 1941).

3. The Gospel of Repentance

IN THE preceding section of this discussion an effort was made to show how the faith that Christ is the revelation of the ultimate meaning of life bears on the doctrine of Christian nurture. In particular, we undertook to show that the underlying assumptions of progressive Protestant nurture are in basic tension with those of Christian faith.

This is, however, only one point at which tension emerges; there are other points of equal importance. One of these concerns the nature of the demand that the Christian gospel makes upon the human subject of redemption. Is the Christian gospel a call to repentance? And if so, what does this imply with respect to man's relation to the Kingdom of God?

In our approach to this aspect of the gospel, let us consider the theme with which Jesus is said to have opened his public ministry. His initial message began: "Repent ye; for the kingdom of heaven is at hand."[1] The key word here is "Repent." Scholars have never agreed upon what Jesus meant by the Kingdom nor upon what is involved in the phrase "at hand"; nevertheless, they all agree that he preached repentance as a necessary condition of participation in the Kingdom. Luke represents Jesus as saying, "Except ye repent, ye shall all likewise perish." The rigorous ideal underlying the call to repentance is revealed in his remark, "Except your righteousness shall exceed the righteousness of the scribes and Pharisees, ye shall in no wise enter into the kingdom of heaven."[2] It is from this perspective that those who heard him were made to wonder whether any person could be saved.

[1]Matt. 4:17. *Cf.* Mark 1:14-15. [2]Matt. 5:20.

In Jesus' call to repentance there is a basic presupposition with respect to man's relation to the Kingdom of God. However one may state the presupposition, it means essentially that human existence is in contradiction with the Kingdom of God, and therefore stands under the judgment of the Kingdom. In this is also signified the fact that man does not, in his "fallen" existence, belong to the Kingdom. The gospel thus confronts man with a radical imperative only because man does not really stand on the inner circle of the Kingdom. As Jesus remarked, "They that are whole have no need of a physician, but they that are sick."[3]

If this be true insight, it is directly pertinent to the present situation in Protestant nurture. For liberal religious nurture in effect presupposes that when man emerges in his empirical existence he is already a member of the Kingdom of God, and needs only more growth from within it. Thus the primary task of Christian nurture in this view is to preserve the child's membership in the Kingdom, rather than to awaken in him the consciousness of the need of repentance as a condition of entrance into it.

In the opinion of some students of American religious thought, Horace Bushnell held essentially this position. Thus William Adams Brown stated in a lecture at the University of Chicago that, according to Bushnell, "the child is by nature Christian and ought to grow up into Christianity naturally as he grows up into citizenship."[4] It is doubtful if Bushnell's position is quite as romantic as Brown seems to think. There is evidence to show that Bushnell did not intend to commit himself to any such doctrine. In his *Christian*

[3]Mark 2:17.
[4]"The Contribution of America to Ecumenical Theology," *The Journal of Religion*, XVIII (1938), p. 271.

Nurture, he definitely criticizes the view that growth in Christian character is a "vegetable process," a mere "onward development." "It involves," he says, "a struggle with evil, a fall and a rescue."[5] This idea is more strongly emphasized in his later writings. "Certain it is," he writes in the second edition of his *Nature and the Supernatural,* "that no individual was ever cleared of sin by development, or restored even proximately to the state of primal order and uprightness."[6] His last work, *Forgiveness and Law,* published in 1874, is even more emphatic in its rejection of the "new gospel of naturalism," according to which "there is nothing to be done for souls in the preparation of character, save by educating, or evolving or developing, what is in them."[7]

Yet it cannot be denied that there is an emphasis in Bushnell's earlier writings that affords some support to Brown's contention. Bushnell's doctrine of Christian nurture was evolved in a period of theological controversy, and the events of the time forced him to emphasize neglected aspects of truth as though they were the whole truth. Thus in effect he served not so much as a theological mediator as a radical innovator. For otherwise he could not have been the religious storm-center that the contemporary accounts show.

The initial issue which engaged Bushnell in controversy arose over the value of revivals of religion.[8] Bushnell saw that the revivalism of his day had become artificial in form and sterile in spiritual result. In particular he recognized that revivalism treated children as mere candidates for future religious experience, after conversion, rather than as beings capable of present religious experience. Against this attitude

[5]P. 23.　　　　[6]Pp. 222 f.　　　　[7]New York, p. 26.
[8]For a brief account of this stormy episode, *see* A. J. W. Myers, *Horace Bushnell and Religious Education* (Boston, 1937), Chaps. II–IV.

of orthodoxy he revolted in the spirit of a crusader. His writings of this period contain epithets which indicate that he was stirred in his emotional depths. In his effort to win his battle against entrenched revivalism Bushnell expounded his views in such fashion as to give a measure of sanction to a position that later liberalism has attributed to him.

Consider, for example, the form in which he states his central thesis of Christian nurture: "That the child is to grow up a Christian, and never know himself as being otherwise." Interpreted in its wider context, it is clear that what Bushnell really means is that the child should be prevented from having a "technical experience" based on a revivalist type of conversion. Dogmatic revivalism held "that the child is to grow up in sin, to be converted after he comes to a mature age." Bushnell would have the child, on the contrary, regarded as having "loved what is good from his earliest years." Taking his thesis on its face, however, it surely carries the implication that the child is to be conscious of himself as naturally Christian.

Significant in this connection also is Bushnell's doctrine of the organic unity of the family.[9] As Bushnell saw it, the great defect of revivalism was that it "makes nothing of the family, and the church, and the organic powers God has constituted as vehicles of grace."[10] To offset this defect he devoted his keenest powers to showing that the child is, by a law of organic connection, unconscious partaker of the spirit and character of the family through a process of nurture that is operative long before he is capable of exercising will and

[9]For an excellent analysis of this aspect of Bushnell's thought, see Luther A. Weigle, "The Christian Ideal of Family Life as Expounded in Horace Bushnell's *Christian Nurture," Religious Education,* XIX (1924), pp. 47–57.
[10]*Christian Nurture,* p. 187.

choice. This occurs, moreover, whether or not the parents design it. "The spirit of the house," he says, "is in the members by nurture, not by teaching, not by any attempt to communicate the same, but because it is the air the children breathe."[11]

Bushnell's main concern is to establish a basis on which to regard the family as an organ of God's regenerative grace. In order to do this he resorts to the biblical idea of covenant, and makes much of the fact that the Jewish Covenant was a family covenant in virtue of which the children became partakers, through the promise, with their parents in the household faith. Both baptism and Church membership he therefore accords the infant on the ground of his organic unity in the faith of the parents. He, to be sure, rejects sacramental baptism; nevertheless, he accepts what he calls "sacramental nurture in the promise."[12] By reason of sacramental nurture, children "are in and of the household of faith, and their growing up is to be in the same."[13] In those families which are united in the covenant with Christ, "the child will be regenerate when he is born."[14] They are thus "as fitly to be counted citizens of the kingdom, as they are to be citizens of the state."[15]

It is this element in Bushnell's thought that became focal in twentieth-century doctrine of religious education, while his later and more realistic appraisal of the human situation has been either ignored or else largely discounted.[16] Let us examine certain recent versions of this earlier Bushnellian emphasis, and, in particular, consider their tendency to ob-

[11]*Ibid.*, p. 101.
[12]*Ibid.*, p. 381, *also* pp. 114–116.   [14]*Ibid.*, p. 198.
[13]*Ibid.*, p. 381.   [15]*Ibid.*, p. 175.
[16]*Cf.* Coe, *The Religion of a Mature Mind*, pp. 305–312; Myers, *Horace Bushnell and Religious Education*, Chap. v.

scure the more radical nature of the gospel of repentance.

(a) As already pointed out, Bushnell sharply dissented from the current view of orthodoxy that the child opens upon life devoid of all holy principle. He did not, even in his earlier writings, deny that the child's nature is "depravated" by parental descent. Yet he properly insisted that it is not sin which the child inherits, but only some prejudice to his harmonious existence, some bias which inclines him to evil. This basis, however, imports personal guilt only after the child enters upon his own self-chosen career and consciously rejects the alternative of good.

But what Bushnell was most concerned to counteract was the orthodox idea that the child is capable of sin, but incapable of good. "Take any scheme of depravity you please," contends Bushnell, "there is yet nothing in it to forbid the possibility that a child should be led, in his first moral act, to cleave unto what is good and right, any more than in the first of his twentieth year."[17] Only unchristian education, he says, "brings up the child for future conversion."[18]

When the twentieth-century movement of religious education emerged, this phase of Bushnell's thought was revived and made basic. The lingering idea of Protestant evangelicalism that the child is alienated from the Kingdom of God was rejected. Children, it was held, are by nature already in possession of a life-principle which requires, not repentance, but spiritual development.[19] The pioneer in this trend of thought, George A. Coe, did not hesitate to assert that the little child is already a member of the Kingdom. "Normal child development takes place entirely within the kingdom of grace."[20] The real question, then, is not, "Will this child

[17]*Christian Nurture*, p. 16.   [18]*Ibid.*, p. 17.
[19]*Cf.* Coe, *Education in Religion and Morals*, p. 46.
[20]*Ibid.*, p. 47.

ever be converted to God? but will he ever be converted away from God?"[21] Coe did not deny that sin is a real element in child existence, but for him the child made his choices between good and evil from within the Kingdom.

This tendency of thought had become widely influential among religious educators of the 1920's. The practical import of this position is, says George H. Betts, that the "child is at the beginning right with God."[22] In this view the function of religious education is to keep the child "right with God," or growing up within the Kingdom. The good seeds of child-nature may be so nourished as to prevent "spiritual coldness or rebellion or purposed evil from which to be reclaimed."[23]

The merit of this emphasis is that it recognizes that the child is not in a religious vacuum; he is never too young to respond either to good or to evil. Its weakness is that it obscures the fact that the child emerges in history as a creature in tension with the Kingdom. In its emphasis on the natural goodness of the child it relaxes the tension by placing the child on the inner circle of the Kingdom. It is therefore as one-sided as the older view that refused to recognize that the child is capable of responding to the call of the Kingdom. Thus in effect it obscures the radical nature of repentance as a condition of participation in the Kingdom.

(b) This brings us to the consideration of another aspect of Bushnell's thought, which, as it has been emphasized in current theory of Protestant nurture, tends to obscure the call to repentance. Bushnell, it was said, was deeply offended by the orthodox practice of teaching children to regard them-

[21]*Ibid.*, p. 55.
[22]*The New Program of Religious Education*, p. 145.
[23]*Ibid.*, p. 47.

selves as sinners, vessels of wrath, and the like. This emphasis, he said, would evoke only morbidity, emotional stress and strain, and thus obstruct healthy growth in Christian character. To set his own point of view in utter contrast to that of orthodoxy, Bushnell boldly asserted that the child should grow up conscious of being, not a sinner, but a Christian, "and never know himself as being otherwise."

This shift in psychological emphasis has exercised a profound influence in American religious life and thought. Whether aware of it or not, Bushnell was expressing a sentiment that was destined to dominate not merely religious thought, but every aspect of American culture. Chronologically, Bushnell marks the transition to romantic America. Liberal religious faith was, to a large degree, the child of this romantic age.

It is typical of this faith that it has always preferred a gospel of health and happiness. Shortly after the advent of the present century, William James, in his Gifford Lectures on *Varieties of Religious Experience,* called attention to the fact that the advance of liberal religion during the previous half century had led to "a victory of healthy-mindedness within the church over the morbid-mindedness."[24] We have a classical example of the product of healthy-minded religious nurture in the late nineteenth century in the person of Edward Everett Hale, one of America's distinguished liberals. Of his childhood religion, Hale says:

I observe, with profound regret, the religious struggles which come into many biographies, as if almost essential to the formation of a hero. I ought to speak of these, to say that any man has an advantage, not to be estimated, who is born, as I was, into a family where the religion is simple and rational; who is trained

[24]New York, 1902, p. 91.

in the theory of such a religion, so that he never knows, for an hour, what these religious or irreligious struggles are. I always knew God loved me, and I was always grateful to him for the world he placed me in. I always liked to tell him so, and was always glad to receive his suggestions to me. . . . A child who is early taught that he is God's child, that he may live and move and have his being in God, and that he has, therefore, infinite strength at hand for the conquering of any difficulty, will take life more easily, and probably will make more of it, than one who is told that he is born the child of wrath and wholly incapable of good.[25]

Present-day theory of religious education is the culmination of the very sort of optimistic nurture of which Hale here speaks so approvingly. From the beginning of this century it has heartily endorsed a religion that is simple and rational; it has discounted a religion of stress and strain; and it has faithfully proclaimed Bushnell's idea that the child should grow up believing himself a Christian.

That orthodox evangelicalism was often guilty of creating in children an exotic religious experience is true. Insofar as modern religious nurture has counteracted the distorting processes of episodic revivalism it has rendered a vital service to the Church. But in its well-intended reaction against revivalism, liberal nurture has fallen a victim to certain illusions of its own. One of these is the belief that the child should *know* himself as a Christian. This is even more unrealistic than the older doctrine that believed that the child should know himself as sinner. For the child who knows himself as sinner at least has a basis for repentance, whereas the child who knows himself as good cannot be expected to feel the need of repentance. The tendency of the latter emphasis is thus to stimulate moral complacency, if not actual

[25]Quoted by James, *Ibid.*, pp. 82 f.

self-righteousness. "Modern man is not well," says Walter M. Horton, "but he refuses to admit that he is sick."[26] Liberal nurture's tendency to educate the child in the consciousness of being Christian is not calculated to cultivate in man the disposition to admit his sickness.

It is possible, to be sure, to exaggerate the sense of sin in human experience, and thereby produce unhealthy morbidity.[27] This is especially true in respect of the young child. That older orthodoxy made its mistakes at this point cannot be denied. But present-day nurture is in no danger here; its danger lies in the propensity to make every child feel that all is sweet and nice within.

4. The Gospel of Deliverance

THE GOSPEL presupposed in Christian nurture is more than the call to repentance; it is also, and supremely, a promise of deliverance from sin by a power greater than ourselves. Jesus associates the call to repentance with the idea of the imminence of the Kingdom of God. The urgency of repentance derives from the fact that the "time is fulfilled, and the Kingdom of heaven is at hand." Implicit in this proclamation of Jesus is the idea that divine deliverance is "at hand" for those who truly repent and turn to God, believing in the gospel. Actual deliverance, however, is recognized as the act of God, not the achievement of man. Repentance is a presupposition of deliverance, and "there shall be joy in heaven over one sinner that repenteth."[1] Nevertheless, the act of deliverance remains a gift of God. Thus Jesus said re-

[26]*The Christian Understanding of Man*, p. 235.
[27]Elliott, *Can Religious Education Be Christian?*, pp. 169–171.
[1]Luke 15:7.

assuringly, "Fear not, little flock, for it is your Father's good pleasure to give you the kingdom."[2]

The same basic idea lies at the center of the Lord's Prayer, although its import is often missed. "And lead us not into temptation, but deliver us from evil, *for thine is the kingdom.*"[3] Here one is made conscious of the fundamental fact that the Kingdom is God's, and that human entrance into it is possible only through the divine deliverance.

The emphasis upon God as deliverer from sin and evil is continued in Paul's teaching. Thus to the Christians at Corinth he writes: "But all things are of God, who reconciled us to himself through Christ."[4] We are not here directly concerned with the problem of the relation of Paul's Christological doctrine to that of the primitive Christian community. It should be said, however, that recent New Testament research sees basic continuity between Paul's doctrine of Christ and that of the Synoptic Gospels.[5] In a recent article, F. C. Grant points out the fact of the diversity of Christological ideas in the New Testament, and yet he admits that the germ of Paul's doctrine may be found in "the more advanced Christology which lies at the basis of the Marcan formulation."[6] Christological continuity between Paul and earlier heralds of the gospel has been clearly substantiated by the research of Frank C. Porter.[7] "With all the diversity of the New Testament writings," says C. H. Dodd,

[2]Luke 12:32.   [3]Matt. 6:13.
[4]II Cor. 5:18.
[5]Nevertheless, Harrison Elliott says Paul "introduced radically new features in the interpretation of Jesus Christ and his relation to the believer." *Can Religious Education be Christian?*, p. 107.
[6]"The Significance of Divergence and Growth in the New Testament," *Christendom*, IV (1939), p. 580.
[7]*The Mind of Christ in Paul* (New York, 1930), pp. 123–127; 143–149; 167–168; 284–286.

"they form a unity in their proclamation of the one gospel."[8] This trend of thought runs contrary to that of a generation ago, which saw in Paul a fundamental departure from the faith of the early Christian Church.

But whatever one may think of Paul's view of Christ in its relation to the interpretation of the Synoptics, one finds in him, as in Jesus, a strong exponent of the idea of theocentric deliverance. Paul himself was an indefatigable laborer under the call of the Kingdom of God; probably no man ever surpassed him in zeal and sacrificial service. Yet no servant of Christ was ever more certain than he that the Kingdom is God's gift, not man's achievement. Out of the depths of arduous struggle he realized that "by the works of the law shall no flesh be justified in his sight."[9]

Paul makes use of many different metaphors to express what takes place, from the divine perspective, when baffled and frustrated man experiences release into the Kingdom of God. Viewed in one context it is *reconciliation;*[10] in another, it is *justification;*[11] in another, it is *adoption;*[12] and in another it is *redemption.*[13] But underlying all these figures of speech is the presupposition that it is God, not man, who redeems human existence from its thralldom and meaninglessness.

Basic though this aspect of the gospel is, yet it forms no central emphasis in the modern theory of Christian nurture. As already indicated, faith in the self-emancipative capacity of man is a primary trait of modern Western culture. It is

[8]*The Apostolic Preaching* (Chicago, 1937), p. 123. Cf. *History and the Gospel*, pp. 52–68. Dibelius, *Gospel Criticism and Christology*, pp. 9–26; Moffatt, *Jesus Christ the Same*, pp. 154–165.
[9]Rom. 3:20.   [10]Rom. 5:11; II Cor. 5:18.
[11]Rom. 3:28.   [12]Rom. 8:15.
[13]I Cor. 1:30; Rom. 3:24.

also, and supremely, the trait of liberal Protestant nurture. Nowhere does this fact reveal itself more clearly than where the problem of deliverance from the power of sin is involved. Let us consider briefly two tendencies of religious-educational thought that bear on this particular element of the Christian gospel.

(*a*) Religious educators of the liberal tradition have always been zealous apostles of "salvation by education." That phrase has taken on a variety of meanings since Coe first made use of it in 1902. But whatever else may be involved in its current use, it means basically belief in rational enlightenment as the resource on which mankind chiefly depends for deliverance from the contradictions and conflicts of human existence. Thus modern man has been exhorted to rely on reason, to have faith in the value of creative intelligence.[14]

This emphasis in religious nurture is, of course, only one phase of a general movement of thought that has characterized liberal culture as a whole ever since its emergence in the eighteenth-century Age of Reason. Liberal culture is rooted in the belief that rational enlightenment is the main factor in the solution of every human ill. It is this confidence in reason that has given modern universal education its main dynamic. It is this faith also that has been a potent factor in the growth of liberal Protestant nurture in our time. Not a few religious educators have believed that a sure way to make religious faith palatable to modern man is to strip it

[14]Thus E. A. Burtt finds Jesus defective as a guide to present-day religious conduct because he "had no appreciation of the value of intelligence as the most dependable human faculty for analyzing the perplexities into which men fall and for providing wise guidance in dealing with them. . . . Repent of your sins, love your neighbor, and have faith in God, is his counsel." *Types of Religious Philosophy* (New York, 1939), pp. 359–360.

of all elements which contradict the scientific mind. This may be illustrated, for example, in the field of biblical criticism, which, incidentally, was of marked interest at the advent of the twentieth-century phase of religious education. Biblical criticism, it was held, would be the means of creating a revival of interest in the Bible, particularly among the "intelligent" reading public. The predicted revival, however, never came.[15]

A similar confidence in the potency of rational enlightenment lies back of the recent enthusiasm for the scientific study of human nature. "Given a little time," wrote E. D. Starbuck in 1923, "religious education can accomplish nearly anything it wants to do with human nature, if only it will gain an accurate knowledge of the laws of mental life, and have the grace to observe them."[16] In the same year, J. M. Artman wrote: "Human nature has discovered a way to change itself."[17] On the background of events since that time, such affirmations seem absurd.

The main root of this faith in salvation by education emerges quite clearly in a book by Clarence R. Skinner. "A liberal believes," he writes, "that when issues are clearly defined, and when men can see the significance of the choice before them, they will cast their lot on the side of moral good and social justice."[18] Thus social injustice exists, presumably, only because men have not yet clearly understood the issues involved in their choices. It is therefore the primary task of educators to define the issues more clearly.

Skinner's basic assumption, however, must not be accepted

[15]Cf. Bower, *The Living Bible,* pp. 4–10.
[16]"What Can Religious Education Do with Human Nature?", *Religious Education,* XVIII (1923), p. 72.
[17]*Idem.* ⌐. 78.
[18]*Liberalism Faces the Future* (New York, 1937), p. 60.

uncritically. It is simply not true that men will necessarily choose the side of social justice if only their ignorance is dispelled. Some of the most notorious offenders against the common good are precisely those who know most clearly the issues involved in their choices. The basic trouble with Skinner's liberalism is that it does not gauge human nature. It reflects a romantic concept of man. In the core of his being man is good, and "on the whole, and over a period of time" man will surely see the good and, of course, do it.[19] Skinner agrees with the sociologists that "so-called sin" is to a large extent the result of faulty environment, cultural lag, or bad heredity. "When certain people are asked to have faith in man there flashes before their minds' eye a concrete instance of the sinfulness and degradation into which some human beings fall, and they become emotionally unable to trust their fellows. They have a fixation which makes them honestly incapable of the liberal point of view."[20] What we need, therefore, "is not so much a revival of the doctrine of sin" as confidence in "collective intelligence."

If only Skinner had a more realistic perspective on human life he would see that collective intelligence is not as simple as his analysis would lead one to suppose. He would perceive that reason in the individual must always reckon with something that is deeper than reason, namely, the urge to live as well as to let live. This urge to self-existence is so strong that it rarely rises to the height of loving one's neighbor as one's self. Furthermore, and more significant in this connection, is the tragic fact that one's rational resources are always more or less corrupted by one's will to self-existence. That is to say, there is a bias in one's mind by reason of the impulse to self-survival. Perfect objectivity in considering the

[19]*Loc. cit.*   [20]*Ibid.*, p. 61.

interests of others is not possible. Thus issues are never "clearly defined" in the sense that one takes a perspective that perfectly transcends the interests of the self. What is true of the individual self is also true of the group. Empirically speaking, there is no such thing as "collective intelligence" in the sense that there is a universal perspective from which mankind judges issues of moral and social good. Empirical society is a composite of groups, larger or smaller, each of which, like the individual selves of which each group is composed, has its own frame of reference. The lack of universality of perspective is evident wherever two or more social groups undertake to adjust their differences. Their efforts to apply the resources of "collective intelligence" quickly reflect the fact that there is no universal mind to apply, but only a congeries of group minds, each of which is rooted in a set of interests that are never fully transcended.

On the other hand, it must be recognized that reason is not entirely circumscribed by the impulse of self-survival. If this were the whole truth, then the human mind would be unable to achieve a perspective from which to criticize the relation of the self to the larger society of selves, and thus would be unable to establish a basis of either personal or social reconstruction. As a matter of fact, the mind is capable of apprehending life from a wider perspective than the self, and even from that of the social group with which the self is most intimately identified. Implicit in the experience of self-consciousness is the experience of other selves. The self thus emerges, not as a totally discrete unit, but as a member of a larger whole with which it is interrelated. The growth of mind in the self, therefore, involves not only the awareness of other selves but also the awareness of the fact that the individual self is intimately related to the growth and destiny of other selves. Reason may thus not only establish a social norm of existence that transcends the impulses of mere self-survival, but it may both reveal and criticize the motives, pretensions, and perspectives of those who thwart life in its more universal dimensions. In this sense, therefore, reason serves as an important resource in personal and social reconstruction.

It is, nevertheless, an illusion to assume that the human self may resolve its tensions between egoistic impulse and social community by a recourse simply to reason. Reason can envisage life in its wider dimensions, and it can establish, within limits, norms of judgment, but it cannot provide the dynamic of redemption. It can reveal the gulf between what is and what ought to be, but it cannot free man from the dominion of that which preserves the gulf. Men to whom the issues "are clearly defined" may still be just those who will not "cast their lot on the side of moral good." Why? A clue to the answer, from the standpoint of Christian faith, is revealed in that frequently quoted passage of Paul: "I see a different law in my members, warring against the law of my mind, and bringing me into captivity under the law of sin which is in my members."[21] Paul's mind envisaged the absolute values of moral existence, but the impulses of his nature failed to rise above the plane of empirical existence. Thus he expressed the experience of every human soul that sees itself from the twofold perspective of both sinner and child of God: "Wretched man that I am! who shall deliver me out of the body of this death?"[22] From this perspective, it is clear that those who say "intelligence is enough" are under an illusion. Not only are they under an

[21]Rom. 7:23.   [22]Rom. 7:24.

illusion, but they, in effect, tend to substitute self-deliverance for divine deliverance.

(*b*) A second emphasis in current theory of liberal nurture runs parallel with that considered in the foregoing section, and has produced equally significant tendencies to obscure the character of the Christian gospel of divine deliverance. This emphasis is expressed in a variety of phrases, but the one that seems to be most inclusive of what is involved is the phrase "creative personality." Its favorite synonym is "creative quest." The underlying assumption on the part of those who use these or similar phrases is that life is rooted in a creative universe; that religion is correspondingly creative; and that human personality is both the supreme value and the primary agent of the creative process.

Whatever else is involved in the idea of creative personality, it signifies that human initiative is the principal factor in personal and social salvation. Our fathers would have called it a gospel of works. For the chief element in a gospel of works is the belief that the Kingdom comes by human action. "We have just one thing to do in life," wrote Coe at the beginning of the century, "and that is to build up the kingdom of God."[23] Speaking more recently from the same standpoint, he writes: "We ourselves must make a new demonstration of ethical love in human relations, or else lose our faith in God."[24] The underlying idea in both of these passages, though widely separated in time, is that human initiative is the root of deliverance; that the Kingdom is deed, not gift.

There is in this mode of thought no adequate recognition of a gospel of theocentric deliverance. Except in the case of

[23] *The Religion of a Mature Mind*, p. 399.
[24] *What Is Christian Education?*, p. 268.

naturalistic liberals, God is not totally ruled out of the process of salvation; nevertheless, He is not recognized as the primary center of salvation. The idea of surrender to a suprahuman Redeemer cannot be found as a primary element in any of the more influential books in twentieth-century theory of religious education.[25]

On the other hand, as already indicated, the newer tendencies of theological thought that emphasize the idea of divine grace in the process of human salvation are being sharply criticized in important circles of religious education.[26] Such tendencies, it is claimed, are authoritarian, supernaturalistic, and world-denying. In particular, these tendencies are alleged to deny the principle of creative personality. They are said to reject the idea that "By creative endeavor he [the child] *can* meet the difficulties that are incidental to superior selfhood."[27]

It is apparent that the Barthian version of current theology does logically tend toward a too complete denial of the place of human action in Christian salvation. Implicit in all forms of unqualified divine sovereignty is the danger that man will be regarded as a too passive factor in divine-human

---

[25]Nor can this idea be said to be given more than incidental attention in the statement of basic philosophy recently issued by the International Council of Religious Education, *Christian Education Today: A Statement of Basic Philosophy*. International Council of Religious Education, 1940, pp. 9–12.

[26]*Cf.* Bower, "Points of Tension Between Progressive Religious Education and Current Theological Trends," *Religious Education,* xxiv (1939), pp. 164–172; Cole, "Where Religious Education and Theology Meet," *Religious Education,* xxxv (1940), pp. 21–24; Elliott, *Can Religious Education be Christian?* Harry C. Munro, "The Returning Sinner Challenges Christian Education," editorial in *The International Journal of Religious Education,* xvii (July–August, 1941), pp. 3–4.

[27]Cole, *op. cit.,* p. 22.

relations. One senses this as a peril in the famous saying of Kierkegaard: "God is in heaven, man upon earth—therefore they cannot well talk together. What man knows is idle chatter, therefore they cannot well talk together. God is love, man is ... a silly little thing."[28] This radical disjunction between God and man lies at the root of Barth's theology. On its terms, as Paul Tillich says, "The kingdom of God is a purely transcendental quantum which is not constructed by men but which comes to men."[29] Furthermore, since human knowledge is only "idle chatter," man cannot recognize the Kingdom even when God does send it!

Early New England theology contained a similar emphasis, but it also contained an important element of correction. An English mentor of the New England Puritans, John Preston, who antedated Kierkegaard by more than two centuries, wrote: "He is in heauen, and wee are on earth; hee the glorious God, we dust and ashes; hee the Creator, and wee but creatures; *and yet he is willing to enter into Couenant, which implyes a kinde of equality betweene vs.*"[30] The first part of this passage sounds like Kierkegaard, but the last clause contains an element that is missing in both Kierkegaard and his twentieth-century followers. It acknowledges that God is sovereign in His Kingdom, yet it denies that God is "wholly other" in His relation to His creatures. Implicit in the idea of covenant is the assumption that man has a responsible part to play both in entering upon, and in preserving, the covenant relation.

[28]*Christian Discourses* (Eng. tr., New York, 1939), p. 323.

[29]"What is Wrong With 'Dialectical' Theology?" *Journal of Religion*, xv (1935), p. 134. This entire article is a brilliant analysis of the strength and the weakness of Barthian theology.

[30]Quoted in Perry Miller, *The New England Mind* (New York, 1939), p. 381. Italics added.

In this idea of covenant is thus the germ of both political and religious democracy. Miller shows clearly that "the federal theologians perfected a philosophy of the Covenant that gave more and more scope to the moral will and put upon men's shoulders the responsibility for their fates."[31] It is true that New England Puritans included in their theology the Calvinist doctrine of "inability," but they were not quietistic in their view of the relation of human action to the coming of the Kingdom. Their prodigious religious labors constitute a denial of any such interpretation. If they saw Pelagianism placing too much confidence in human works, they also saw Antinomianism underestimating the value of human works. They could endorse neither extreme, "when *virtus* is in the middle."[32]

With rare exceptions, American Protestantism always has been characterized by a more or less moralistic and self-help gospel. The germ of moral activism that is found in early Puritan covenant theology has been nurtured by many different forces in the development of Amercian culture. There is thus little danger that the Barthian version of the gospel will establish itself in American culture and in the theory of Protestant nurture. The danger is rather that the religious educator will take more seriously Emerson's gospel of self-reliance than he will the gospel according to Paul: "By grace have ye been saved through faith; and that not of yourselves, it is the gift of God."[33]

[31]*Ibid.*, p. 393.　　　[32]*Ibid.*, p. 372.　　　[33]Eph. 2:8.

CHAPTER FIVE

THE CHURCH: COMMUNITY OF
CHRISTIAN NURTURE

CHRISTIAN nurture, like every other process of shared experience, presupposes a medium of nurture. For Christian faith, this medium is the Church. The Church as an organized body is not, of course, the only medium of religious nurture; for Christian experience may be shared through many different modes of collective behavior. Nevertheless, it is a significant fact that Christians have always regarded the Church as the supreme society through which to experience the reality of the gospel and to mediate it to others.

For this reason it is lamentable that the nature of the Church should not be more clearly understood by Christians. American Protesants are particularly vague in their conception of the Church, despite the fact that there is a considerable body of literature produced annually on the subject. Nowhere is this vagueness of view more evident than among religious educators. Religious educators seem to have been less concerned with the nature of the Church than any other professional group in religion. This is true in spite of the fact that recent years have witnessed an increasing use of the term "church-centered" in educational literature.

At least five factors lie back of this attitude. In the first place, the core-agency of Christian nurture in the local

Church, the Sunday-school, always has been more or less independent of the Church, even though housed and fostered by the Church. Paul H. Vieth has accurately described the situation: "It may be said of the school of religion that it has been *in* the church but not *of* the church."[1] A closer relation between Church and school has been brought about in recent years,[2] but nothing like real integration has yet taken place in most local churches. Religious educators in local churches have, under these conditions, tended to concern themselves with "educational" activities as over against "Church" activities. The creation of the office of director of religious education in the local church as distinct from that of pastor or minister served to accentuate the difference between the Church and "the church school."

A second factor is that the twentieth-century theory of religious nurture is derived largely from theories of education that are apposite to the secular school. These theories reflect no interest in the Church as a distinctive community of nurture. On the other hand, they have no doubt fostered the recent tendency to interpret the Church in terms of "a school in religious living." The implication in this tendency is that the term school embodies a more vital meaning for Christian nurture than the term church, which is unfortunate.

A third factor lies in the sharp distinction that has been drawn between the Church and the Kingdom of God, with

[1] *Objectives in Religious Education* (New York, 1930), p. 234.

[2] National leaders in religious education have often urged that the entire work of the Church be conceived as an educational enterprise. *See,* for example, L. A. Weigle and J. H. Oldham, "A Preliminary Paper," in report of the Jerusalem Meeting of the International Missionary Council, 1928, Vol. II: *Religious Education,* p. 4; *Christian Education Today, A Statement of Basic Philosophy* (International Council of Religious Education, 1940), p. 17.

the result that the former has often been regarded as merely instrumental to the latter. Liberal Protestantism, and notably the social-gospel phase, has centered its emphasis on the Kingdom of God, and it has reflected almost constant fear that the historical Church would obscure the vision of the Kingdom.[3] In this emphasis on the Kingdom liberals, to be sure, have claimed the support of Jesus. Thus, in 1893, A. M. Fairbairn wrote: "How did Jesus conceive and describe His society? . . . His familiar phrase was not 'the Church,' but 'the kingdom of heaven' or 'of God,' or simply 'My kingdom.' The mere figures are significant: the term 'kingdom' is used in the Gospels to denote His society 112 times, and almost always by Himself; but 'Church' only twice."[4] On the basis of this analysis Fairbairn concluded that the social ideal of Jesus was the Kingdom, not the Church.[5] Fairbairn's attitude has been characteristic of liberal Protestants throughout the twentieth century. Whatever may be the merits of this emphasis it is clear that it has tended to relegate the Church to a place of secondary importance.

A fourth factor lies in the religious educator's preoccupation with "religion" or "religious experience" in contrast to the institutional forms of religion. In general, he fears the deadening effect of the Church upon religion, although he admits the necessity of the organized Church. The atti-

---

[3]Where the older social gospel placed its primary emphasis is implicit in Rauschenbusch's remark, "The Church grows old; the Kingdom is ever young." *A Theology for the Social Gospel*, pp. 129 f. It is significant, however, that the newer social-gospel trend of thought is giving a much larger recognition to the place of the Church. *See*, for example, F. Ernest Johnson's illuminating book, *The Social Gospel Re-examined* (New York, 1940), Chap. iv.

[4]*The Place of Christ in Modern Theology* (New York, 1893), p. 515.

[5]*Ibid.*, p. 516.

tude of not a few leaders in religious education is correctly expressed by the Wiemans: "A church without religion is much more dangerous than is religion without a church."[6] Thus while the Church must be tolerated, it must not be allowed to obstruct one's loyalty to religion. One way to prevent obstruction is to insist that the Church is purely instrumental in the process of religious growth. In the words of Soares, "The church is, after all, only a means to an end."[7]

A fifth factor, and a most important one, derives from the fact that the religious educator, like large numbers of American Protestants, belongs to a religious tradition which Troeltsch has called the sect-type. The sect-type of Protestantism, in distinction to the church-type, is characterized by an emphasis upon experimental religion, and upon the Church as a fellowship of voluntarily committed believers. Implicit in this emphasis is a tendency to minimize the institutional aspect of Christianity. It is out of this general tradition that liberal Protestant nurture has sprung. The sect-type of American Protestantism has furnished the principal leadership in the contemporary movement in religious education.

Considering the combined influence of these five factors, it is not surprising that the current philosophy of liberal nurture gives no direct attention to the Christian doctrine of the Church. In this respect, of course, religious education has not been essentially different from other aspects of American Christianity. Nevertheless, it is significant that the present emerging interest in achieving a more adequate conception of the Church has met as yet with no particular enthusiasm among religious educators as a group. On the contrary, this newer tendency of Christian thought is meeting with

[6]*Normative Psychology of Religion*, p. 502.
[7]*Religious Education*, p. 257.

active opposition in certain circles. Some profess to see in it a subtle method to enslave religion in a new form of authoritarianism; some look upon it as a mode of ecclesiastical introversion; and others regard it as a sign of escape from the realities of the current social crisis.

It is possible, to be sure, that the present concern to discover the deeper meaning of the Church may, in some cases, result in an unrealistic attitude toward society and toward religion. Crucial periods in the world's life and thought usually stimulate false attitudes toward religion as well as true ones. There is no guarantee that only true conceptions and ideals will emerge in the present confusing situation. This is true in respect of the present movement to rethink the doctrine of the Christian Church; it is quite likely that erroneous and misleading doctrines will arise. Yet this is in itself no reason why one should decline to re-examine the meaning of an essential aspect of the Christian faith.

That there is a rising tide of interest in the nature of the Church is self-evident. The topic has come to the surface in all the recent ecumenical conferences, and it is the central theme of a growing number of important books.[8] It appears to be a subject that will continue to occupy much of the best theological thought of the world.[9] It is the writer's conviction that Christian educators, along with other groups, should participate actively in this effort to come to a more basic understanding of the idea of the Church.

No attempt is made in this chapter to analyze or compare the various historical doctrines of the Church. Nor is any

---

[8]For example, Nels Ferré, *The Christian Fellowship;* C. C. Morrison, *What Is Christianity?* (Chicago, 1940); S. Mathews, *The Church and the Christian* (New York, 1938); R. Newton Flew, *Jesus and His Church* (London, 1938).

[9]*Cf.* Flew, "Our Next Task," *Christendom,* IV (1939), pp. 57–67.

effort made to develop a balanced and comprehensive conception of the Church. Our primary purpose is rather to focus attention upon certain basic aspects of the Christian doctrine of the Church that are either neglected or else inadequately treated in modern theory of religious education.

1. Community of the Divine Initiative

A BASIC presupposition of the Church is community. Without community or fellowship there could be no Christian Church. Nevertheless, the principle of community, as such, does not provide a clue to the distinctive character of the Church; for all kinds of collective life involve community of thought and action in the creation and transmission of social values. It is thus not community, *per se,* but a particular sort of community that distinguishes the Church from all other modes of associated life. What, then, are the distinguishing marks of that type of community which constitutes the Church?

In the first place, the Church claims to be a distinctive community in respect of its origin. It is the Christian faith that the Church emerged in history, not through the anticipation of man but through the antecedent determination of God. It believes itself to have come into being through the creative act of the Divine Initiative, as manifested in the Word made flesh in Jesus Christ. The substance of this faith was succinctly expressed by the Second World Conference on Faith and Order. "We all agree," says the Conference, "that the Christian Church is constituted by the eternal Word of God made man in Christ and is always vitalized by his Holy Spirit."[1]

[1] *The Second World Conference on Faith and Order,* ed. Leonard Hodgson (London, 1938), p. 230.

That the origin of the Christian community is inseparably associated with the life, death, and resurrection of Jesus Christ is acknowledged by all students of the early Church. Whether Jesus himself formally founded the Church is a question on which Protestant thought continues to be divided. An increasing number of Protestant thinkers, however, believe that Jesus was in some essential sense founder of the Christian Church.[2] "The crowning work of Jesus," writes W. M. Horton, "was the founding of the Church."[3] In a closely reasoned work, *Jesus and His Church,* Flew takes the position that Jesus definitely envisaged the emergence of the Church in terms of "a community of a new kind."[4]

It is probably true that Jesus did not regard himself as founder of the Christian Church in a formal sense. Nevertheless, he became the center of a community which in essence constituted the Church. The immediate fruit of Jesus' ministry was neither a New Testament nor a formal institution. It was, rather, a dynamic fellowship whose creative center was God as incarnated in Christ. This fellowship underwent a process of growth in its understanding of Jesus Christ, and also in its apprehension of its nature and mission under Christ's leadership. Pentecost is, of course, the event that marked what is historically regarded as the formal birthday of the Christian Church. For it was on this occasion that the little group of Christ's followers experienced an extraordinary consciousness of community with Christ in the Holy Spirit. Nevertheless, the Church in its

[2] *Cf.* W. A. Visser 't Hooft and J. H. Oldham, *The Church and Its Function in Society* (Chicago, 1939), p. 14.

[3] *Realistic Theology,* p. 140.

[4] P. 48. *Cf.* C. C. Morrison, *What Is Christianity?* pp. 125–127, 144; H. F. Rall, *Christianity* (New York, 1940), pp. 47–51.

essence had its beginning long before that. Thus A. E. Garvie is correct when he says that <u>Pentecost, strictly speaking, marks not the birthday of the Church, but its baptism.</u>[5]

The Church as the community of the early Christians reveals a twofold consciousness. On the one hand, the Christian community was aware of its religious continuity with the Jewish Church, with the Old Israel. "There can be no question at all," says Archbishop William Temple, "that the Church in the beginning of its Christian period regarded itself as continuous with and indeed identical with that Church of the Old Covenant which was known by the name of Israel."[6] On the other hand, the early Christians were also conscious of a new element in their faith. This new element was the ardent faith that the promised Messiah had already entered history in the person of Jesus Christ, and that this same Christ would also shortly return to consummate the Kingdom of God.[7] This awareness of being a New Israel was doubtless a growing experience; yet when it attained full fruition, the New Israel was probably more aware of its difference from than of its likeness to the Israel of the Old Covenant.[8] Thus Hans Lietzmann, a recognized authority on the history of the early Church, writes: "The young religious society had an astonishingly clear consciousness of

[5]"The Reunion of the Churches: Some Fundamental Problems," *Christendom,* v (1940), p. 66.

[6]*The Church and Its Teaching Today* (New York, 1936), p. 6.

[7]*See* Hans Lietzmann, *The Beginnings of the Christian Church* (Eng. tr., London and New York, 1937), p. 79.

[8]For recent and instructive accounts of the process by which the New Israel developed into a self-conscious community, *see* Donald W. Riddle, *The Gospels, Their Origin and Growth* (Chicago, 1939), Chaps. x–xi; Frederick C. Grant, "The Nature of the Church: Historical Origins," *Anglican Theological Review,* xxi (1939), pp. 190–204; Floyd V. Filson, "The Separation of Christianity from Judaism," *Anglican Theological Review,* xxi (1939), pp. 171–185.

its own significance as a completely new element that had entered history and had destroyed the old criteria."[9] Unless some such conviction had finally dawned, it is not easy to account for the ultimate separation of the two Israels.

At the heart of this New Israel was a growing assurance that God through Christ had offered mankind a new center of fellowship. Peter's historic discourse expresses the gist of that faith: "This Jesus did God raise up, whereof we all are witnesses. Being therefore by the right hand of God exalted, and having received of the Father the promise of the Holy Spirit, he hath poured forth this, which ye see and hear."[10] The point of emphasis in this connection is revealed in Peter's affirmation, "He hath poured forth this." The dynamic of the new fellowship is thus the Holy Spirit, which the early Christians recognized as the gracious gift of God.

This fundamental element of the community of the Church is far from being a central emphasis in modern religious nurture, even though in some circles the Church is vaguely spoken of as a divine institution. To be sure, liberal educators lay much stress upon fellowship as being basic in the process of moral and religious growth. This is notably true of those who, with the aid of modern social science, lay primary emphasis upon the social foundations of personality. Yet the idea of the Church as a fellowship that arose through the Divine Initiative in Jesus Christ remains obscure, or at least undeveloped. On the other hand, the tendency to regard the Church as an emergent of the social process has been pronounced, especially in left-wing circles of liberal Protestantism. This tendency was partly a reaction against a supernaturalistic doctrine of the Church, which,

[9] *Op. cit.*, p. 64.   [10] Acts 2:32–33.

in its extreme form, largely discounted the human or social aspect of the Church. This general point of view was recently vigorously reaffirmed by Shailer Mathews, who manifestly is disturbed over the idea of the Church that has dominated recent ecumenical conferences.[11] "The organization and function of a church," says Mathews, "are not revealed from heaven but are aspects of that social behavior which the word Christianity connotes."[12]

A similar point of view is reflected in Bower's interpretation of the nature of the Church. For him as for Mathews, Christianity "is not something given," but is essentially a social movement.[13] From this point of view the Church is the embodiment of a movement that is also essentially social.[14] Bower refers vaguely to "those spiritual resources that reside in and beyond the group"; but precisely what the nature of those forces is in relation to the emergence and sustenance of the Christian Church is not made explicit.

This emphasis upon the social side of the Church contains a truth that should be given full recognition. That the Church as a reality of history emerges within the social matrix and mediates its message through existing patterns of human culture is a fact which must be fully accepted in all its implications. To emerge meaningfully within history, the Church must necessarily partake of the relative forms of imperfect society. Only thus in fact would Christian nurture be at all possible. To recognize the full significance of this empirical side of the Church will save Christian nurture from a type of dogmatism and obscurantism that has

[11]*The Church and the Christian,* pp. 4–7.
[12]*Ibid.,* p. 10. Cf. *Creative Christianity* (Nashville, 1935), p. 66.
[13]*The Church at Work in the Modern World,* p. 1.
[14]*Ibid.,* p. 272. Cf. *The Curriculum of Religious Education,* pp. 230–231.

all too often marred the history of the Christian community.

But even when this empirical aspect of the Church is fully recognized, there remains the problem of the ultimate source of the Christian fellowship. <u>The Church is something more than merely a group of like-minded persons who get together and form a social fellowship.</u> The Church is, for faith, the unique creation of God in Christ and in the Holy Spirit. This is the basis of its being a true *koinonia,* a true community of the Spirit. <u>Human creatures are bound together in Christian fellowship, but the uniting bond of that fellowship is God-given.</u> Human creatures experience fellowship with one another in the Spirit, but they do not create the Spirit. <u>Human culture fashions the forms through which the Christian fellowship nurtures human creatures, but culture does not generate the living reality that sustains the forms.</u>

It thus becomes clear that both the social and the suprasocial aspects of the Church must be recognized in any adequate account of the emergence of the Christian fellowship. Recognition of the social or empirical element of the Church will save Christian educators from any tendency to identify the Kingdom of God and the Church; while, on the other hand, recognition of the supra-social element of the Church will save Christian educators from the tendency to identify the Church with any sort of ideal social group.

2. *Community of the Ultimate Fulfilment of Life*

A SECOND aspect of the Church as a distinctive community of nurture is closely related to the first; in fact, it may be conceived as its correlative. As the Church is a community whose creative source transcends the empirical world-process, so the Church is a community whose ultimate fulfilment points beyond the plane of historical existence. If the Church has its ultimate origin in the Kingdom of God, it has also its ultimate consummation only in the Kingdom of God. Thus the Christian prays, "Thy Kingdom come." In this he admits that the Kingdom is the normative reality of the Church and of Christian nurture. In this he also admits that the historical Church is in disparity with the Kingdom, and therefore is under its judgment.

At this point the question naturally arises, may the Christian community ever hope to experience perfect meaning and fulfilment on the plane of historical existence? Or is the Church doomed to an existence that will always remain as something less than the perfection of the Kingdom? If one consults past history for an answer, it is clear that the Church as an empirical reality has always fallen short of the perfection of the absolute Kingdom. It is a common tendency to regard the Church of the early Christians as being without spot or wrinkle; but any realistic reading of the letters of Paul and the book of Acts will easily dispel this illusion. Party cries, petty jealousies, and group antagonisms mar the fellowship of the earliest Christian communities. In the closing book of the New Testament, the Apocalypse of John, we have a sharp arraignment of "the seven churches that are in Asia." John reminds these churches that Christ "made us to be a kingdom," yet he also sadly confesses that they fall far short of that ideal. Thus from the very beginning the Church reveals its contradictory or ambivalent character. The Church claims to be the Body of Christ; nevertheless, it knows itself to be a very imperfect body. This has been the experience of the Church throughout its checkered history. The Church has never stood exclusively over against the world; it has always been partly of the world.

But what of the future? May the Church of tomorrow expect to overcome this ambivalent or contradictory existence? May it ever hope to nurture mankind into the perfect fullness of Christian fellowship within the matrix of human culture? May the Christian community, in other words, become the Kingdom of God? The tendency of liberalism, as already seen, has been rather optimistic in its answer. Under the influence of the modern evolutionary idea of progress, the hope of the social realization of the Kingdom became dominant. Those who espoused "the religion of democracy" were especially enamored of this hope. Only an otherworldly religion, they thought, could hinder the steady progress of the coming Kingdom.[1]

Recent religious thought, however, reveals a pronounced reaction against this one-sided optimism. A deeper insight into the complexities of human society on the one hand and a more penetrating insight into the character of the Kingdom of God on the other hand lies at the root of this change in outlook. With a realistic eye on the social scene, Reinhold Niebuhr writes: "There is no hope of overcoming the contradictions, in which life stands, in history."[2] From the point of view of the absolute ethic of the Kingdom, C. H. Dodd tells us that it is an illusion to suppose "that ever in this world we could fulfil these precepts of Jesus with the absoluteness that is inherent in them."[3]

In light of current religious thought, therefore, it is unrealistic for the Church to expect to nurture human life into

[1]*Cf.*, for example, A. C. McGiffert, "Democracy and Religion," *Religious Education*, xiv (1919), p. 160.

[2]*Beyond Tragedy* (New York, 1937), p. 23. *Cf.* W. M. Horton, *Realistic Theology*, p. 156.

[3]*History and the Gospel*, p. 127. *Cf.* Martin Dibelius, *The Sermon on the Mount* (New York, 1940), Chap. IV, and pp. 65, 87, 94, 97–99.

absolute fulfilment of Christian fellowship on the plane of empirical existence. The new strain of Christian teaching thus agrees with the *Imitation* that "All perfection in this life has some imperfection mixed with it, and all our knowledge is not without some darkness."[4] The Church of history, in other words, will always be something less than the perfect community of the Kingdom of God, as will also society of which the Church forms an organic part. The perfect fellowship of the Kingdom is the symbol of "the end" of history.[5] In this sense, therefore, the faith of the Church is undeniably otherworldly.

This emphasis is, however, easily subject to perversion. If the liberalism of yesterday overrated the possibilities of Christian fellowship within historic society, current religious thought is inclined in some circles to underrate its possibilities. This temper of spirit manifested itself, for example, at the world gathering of the Churches at Madras in 1938. The German delegates, taking issue with the prevailing sentiment of the Conference, said, "But being between the times, the Church has not to bring into force a social program for a renewed world order, or even a Christian state."[6]

Precisely this attitude found expression in the most influential theologian of the Old South, James H. Thornwell. As against humanitarians of the North who wanted to abolish chattel slavery, Thornwell contended that it was not the mission of the Church "to construct society afresh, . . . to rearrange the distribution of its classes, or to change the forms

[4]Thomas à Kempis, *The Imitation of Christ,* ed. Albert Hyma (New York, 1927), i, iii, 8.

[5]*Cf.* Dodd, *op. cit.,* pp. 65–66; Niebuhr, *op. cit.,* pp. 21–24.

[6]*The World Mission of the Church: Findings and Recommendations of the International Missionary Council* (New York, 1938), p. 151.

of its political constitutions." Nor, he continued, is it the province of the Church "to build asylums for the needy or insane."[7] These problems are the result of man's "fallen state" and the Church "must leave them to the Providence of God."

In both of these statements, though widely separated in time, there is reflected a theology that in effect sanctions the existing structure of society in the name of an absolutely transcendent Kingdom of God. The German group quite frankly admitted that since "we live as citizens of two different orders," the natural order must be endured in its fallen condition until the Second Advent.[8] The Church, to be sure, "cannot pass by the sufferings of the world"; it must heal the sick, comfort the downtrodden, and inspire sacrificial acts of mercy. Yet the Church as an "interim-body" must not expect a fundamentally reconstructed social order. Likewise Thornwell stressed the importance of showing kindness to the individual slave; and he sincerely enjoined masters to make provision for the religious instruction of their slaves, who, no less than white people, possessed immortal souls that should be "saved." He preached that all souls, black as well as white, were equal before God; yet he stoutly denied that this fact involved any change in the unequal status of the slave on earth. For him, as for the German group at Madras, the world of history and the world of the Kingdom of God constitute two distinct realms.

Both of these cases, therefore, show how the Church may tacitly justify social evil in the name of a falsely conceived otherworldly Kingdom of God. On any such basis the Church can, on the one hand, easily withdraw from the so-

[7]*Collected Writings,* ed. J. B. Adger and J. L. Girardeau (Richmond, 1872), Vol. IV, p. 383.
[8]*The World Mission of the Church,* p. 150.

cial struggle and preach a pietistic gospel, or, on the other hand, it can as easily immerse itself in the social struggle without any acute awareness of the judgment of the Kingdom of God upon the Christian community. In either case, however, the Church surrenders its ambivalent or paradoxical character and thus ceases to be a realistic community of Christian nurture.

A realistic Christian nurture, then, is not at liberty to dissolve the ethical tension that exists between the Church and the Kingdom of God, either by way of an optimistic liberalism that tends to equate the Kingdom with an ideal social community, or by way of a pessimistic dualism that transfers the realm of the Kingdom to a world totally outside the process of human history. The world of social history is neither a demonic vacuum nor is it the plane on which perfection of fellowship is achieved. The Church is a community that nurtures mankind in the faith that even though perfect fellowship may not be realized on the plane of human history, yet history is the scene in which the Kingdom is at work among men, and may be indefinitely approximated. The Church is also a community that lives in the faith that ultimate fulfilment of life in the Kingdom of God is assured.

3. *The Christian Center of Community*

A THIRD distinctive element of the Church concerns the unifying center of Christian fellowship. There has never been any doubt in the mind of the Christian movement that the Church is, in theory, one community. The basis of the Church's unity was clearly seen by Paul. Hearing that certain sectaries at Corinth were saying, "I am of Paul; and I of Apollos; and I of Cephas; and I of Christ," Paul rightly asked, "Is Christ divided?"[1] Toward the close of his life, when Paul had become wistful that the faithful at Ephesus might not preserve the "unity of the Spirit," he reminded them that there was but "one Lord, one faith, one baptism, one God and Father of all, who is over all, and through all, and in all."[2]

Paul here clearly reveals that the Church is a community whose locus of unity is in "one Lord." It is this Christocentric bond of the Church that supremely distinguishes the character of Christian community from contemporary types of community. Even though our age is witnessing the rise of new sorts of communities, these communities center their unifying bond in such realities as nation, class, or race. Yet the more completely these new forms of community integrate themselves around these empirical realities, the more precarious human existence becomes. It therefore seems that whenever an empirical reality is treated as though it were the final or ultimate center of existence, devotees of that center sow the seeds of moral disintegration. Unless these empirical entities therefore can find a center beyond themselves, the future of world community is dark.

It is this truth which the Church needs to declare in this tragic moment of the world's life. Yet it is a fact that the empirical condition of the Church itself is such that its message is seriously weakened. It is the Church's faith that it is one community; nevertheless, the churches of history obscure or deny that faith. The forces that have created tension within the world have also created tension within the empirical community of the Church. It is this condition that

[1] I Cor. 1:12–13. Moffatt suggestively translates Paul's question, "Is Christ parcelled out?"
[2] Eph. 4:4–6.

seriously weakens the nurturing power of the Church. The empirical realities of the Church are primary factors in Christian nurture. Especially is this true in the case of children, whose attitudes and value-judgments are so largely formed by the experiences and activities of the adult members of the religious community. If the empirical realities of adult life contradict the essential oneness of the Church of Christ, the nurture of the young will inevitably fall short of Christian nurture.

"The church," says Kraemer, "ought always to be aware of its condition of crisis on account of the abiding tension between its essential nature and its empirical condition."[3] If the Church of today is not fully awake to its condition of crisis as a community of nurture, it is by no means because the Church is free from the entanglements of the world. The reason seems to lie mostly in the fact that the Church has lost consciousness of its unity in Jesus Christ.

Yet there is ground for hope in the fact that the Church is able to recognize to some extent the nature of the forces that serve to split her empirical community. This in itself is a sign that the Church has not yet lost all awareness of its essential center of unity in Christ. To recognize the forces of bondage does not in itself emancipate the Church, but at least it is a preliminary step in the right direction. Even though the Church cannot rescue itself, it yet must recognize its sources of disunity or it will never be rescued.

Of the factors creating empirical disunity in the Church as a nurturing community, four will be briefly analyzed. They are not the only factors, but they are illustrative of the crisis in which the Church finds itself in our time.

[3]H. Kraemer, *The Christian Message in a Non-Christian World* (New York, 1938), pp. 24–25.

(*a*) In its essential being as the Body of Christ, the Church is a community of nurture which cannot recognize men as economic men, but only as persons made in the image of God and therefore as equal sons of the same Father. To be sure, economic values are important values in the growth of persons; but they are not normative in the value-scale of the Christian faith.

Yet it cannot be denied that modern Western culture, of which religion is an integral part, is far from innocent at this point. In the rise of modern Western culture, economic interests not only became autonomous in relation to other human interests; but by a subtle process, and due to numerous factors, economic interests tended to become normative in the scale of social values. In other words, economic life was exalted to the apex of life's meaning. Thus the medieval synthesis was not only dissolved, but the dissolution resulted in the emergence of a new center of meaning and value. In effect a new religion emerged, the religion of the economic man.

That the Church has participated in this modern cultural process of the perversion of life's true center of value and meaning is well authenticated:[4] This participation has involved both positive and negative aspects. Negatively, the Church encouraged the perversion by treating economic relations as if such relations were beyond its orbit of concern; and positively, by an uncritical assimilation of the ethic of the economic man. Thus the victory of the economic virtues was, with rare and indecisive exceptions, unhampered by modern religion. The final result of what might be called modern religion's Great Surrender was succinctly summed

[4]*See,* for example, R. H. Tawney, *Religion and the Rise of Capitalism* (London and New York, 1926).

up by R. H. Tawney. In the closing statement of his great
work, *Religion and the Rise of Capitalism,* Tawney writes:
"From a spiritual being, who, in order to survive, must de-
vote a reasonable attention to economic interests, man seems
sometimes to have become an economic animal, who will be
prudent, nevertheless, if he takes due precautions to assure
his spiritual well-being."[5]

It is not our concern here to deal with the general effects
of this perversion, but rather to call attention to the way in
which it has affected the Church as a community of nurture.
That there is a definite effect can hardly be doubted. To the
extent that the Church has absorbed the ethic of the economic man, the Church has opened the door to a tacit alli-
ance with some particular economic interest of the social
order. Let us state the same idea in another fashion. The
Church which loses its supra-economical center of community will tend to locate its empirical center not merely in economic values in general, but in some particular economic
class or group. Thus a Church which capitulates to the economic man is in danger of capitulating also to the class man.
Out of this arises a class Church. A class Church, however,
splits the empirical community into rival communities and
destroys the spiritual and the cultural basis of Christian nurture.

On the assumption that this is true, Christian educators
have reason to view with serious concern an official statement made in 1936 by a group of American churchmen of
wide experience. Writing on the state of the Church in
America, they said: "Another entanglement of the church
today which impresses us as a matter of grave concern is its
assimilation of the assumptions and ideals of the comfortable

[5]*Ibid.,* p. 279.

middle class. . . . They [the churches] are likely to look, and very often do look, with hesitation and fear upon the struggle of the masses for better conditions of life. . . . The ethical assumptions and attitudes of the members of these churches seem to be dominated by the business and social connections of the members rather than by the judgments of God upon our human order set forth in the Scriptures."[6]

The religious situation described by these churchmen has, of course, its historical antecedents. Of some of these, Arthur E. Holt, in his Rauschenbusch Lectures, writes: "Realism compels us to record such facts as that, in the time of Alexander Hamilton and Thomas Jefferson, the actions of the Connecticut clergy justified the reproach that they were the 'Cossacks of the Federalist party'; and that, in the conflict between Jackson and Adams, the clergy joined the bankers in supporting Adams. The Populist struggle which culminated in the battle between Bryan and McKinley found the metropolitan clergy—Catholic, Jewish and Protestant, from Chicago to the Atlantic coast—voting the way Mark Hanna wanted them to vote."[7]

Thus it is clear that class tendencies in the Church are not peculiar to the contemporary scene. Yet it can hardly be denied that the issue of class tension in religion today is much more acute than it has been in any other period of American culture, owing to the unprecedented nature of the social and economic crisis through which we are now passing. The burgeoning consequences of the second World War, both immediate and remote, will intensify the growing

[6]Albert W. Beaven, *et al.,* "The State of the Church," *The Christian Century,* LIII (1936), p. 1746. For expression of a similar conviction, see "The State of the Church," *Christendom,* VI (Spring, 1941), pp. 211–212.

[7]*This Nation under God* (Chicago, 1939), p. 110.

tensions within as well as without the churches. The accelerated rate at which religious cult-movements are emerging among the depressed classes in America is authentic evidence that these classes are definitely outside the pale of the middle-class Church.

The implications of this situation for Christian nurture are clear. If, as Coe says, "a church makes its members more than the members make the church,"[8] then it seems reasonable to suppose that the processes of nurture in the middle-class Church of today are tending to mold the mind of the young in terms of a class religion. Thus the nurture of the present-day Church is partly the source of the very tensions which it seeks to resolve.

(b) A second factor which introduces tension into the community of Christian nurture is racialism. Racial tension is arising with new intensity in all areas of Western culture, a fact due in large measure to the rapid collapse of established modes of life and thought. It is especially acute in Germany, but it is by no means an incidental factor in the experience of other countries, including our own. If America has been the "melting pot of the races," she has also been the subject of almost continuous racial tensions, a fact which shows that the various races have never been really melted together. The sensitiveness to race in America is clearly gauged, for example, by the delicacy with which the public schools must deal with it.[9] With respect to the relations between white and colored, Coe says, "There is enough silence in the textbooks to deafen any one who has sensitive ears."[10]

[8] *A Social Theory of Religious Education*, p. 85.
[9] *Cf.* Howard K. Beale, *Are American Teachers Free? Report of the Commission on Social Studies of the American Historical Association* (New York, 1936), pp. 145–149; 196–197.
[10] *Educating for Citizenship*, p. 175.

The main reason for this silence is that the issue involved is so temper-upsetting that the democratic and moral health of American culture is hardly robust enough to deal with it.

The virus of race is in the bloodstream of American religion as well as in other aspects of our culture. That the faith of the Church is supra-racial is clear. In the one community of Christ the contradictions of race are transcended. "For in Christ Jesus you are all sons of God. . . . There is no room for 'Jew' and 'Greek'; there is no room for 'slave' and 'freeman.' "[11]

Viewed from this perspective men are never race men; they are creatures bearing the divine image, and are thus sons of a common fellowship in the one body of Christ. Nevertheless, this one body is riven in its empirical existence by race. Our historic denominationalism is itself in part a monument to the racialization of the Christian community. Even where reunions of formerly separated bodies are taking place, as in the merger of the three branches of American Methodism,[12] they usually involve significant and tragic concessions to racialism. Biracialism in the Christian community has been the accepted principle in the South for generations, although it is only since the Civil War that it has attained practical universality. But, unfortunately, Negro migrations into the North and West in large numbers are resulting in marked tendencies to reproduce the biracial religious patterns of the South.

In the sphere of race, as in that of economics, one can see what takes place in human life when the unity of the Christian community loses its supra-social center. If the

[11]Gal. 3:26-28. Goodspeed tr.
[12]See Francis J. McConnell, "Methodist Reunion," *Christendom*, IV (1939), pp. 361-362.

principle of race is allowed to become normative, the door is opened to racial distinctions of varying degrees, not merely distinctions as between white and colored, but also as between Jew and Gentile, Aryan and non-Aryan. The natural result is the emergence of racial religions. Thus it is not difficult to understand how Herr Rosenberg can say that "the German people is the subject, not of original sin, but of original nobility."[13] Understandable, too, is Hitler's vaunt that the Aryan is the race with whom "all human creations originate."[14] The Nazi premise that race-value is the normative value of community[15] ends not merely with the deification of humanity, but with the absolutizing of a particular human community over all other communities. Implicit in this doctrine is the idea that the self-styled superior race has the right, indeed the duty, to subjugate all other racial communities. Terrible as Nazism may be, it at least has the virtue of demonstrating the logical outcome of a racial theory of human society.

That Nazism should seek to distort or to destroy the Christian ethic of human equality is to be expected, for Christianity is in irreconcilable conflict with the basic premise of Nazism. Without a fundamental change in one or the other it is inconceivable that an equilibrium can be established between National Socialism and Christianity. Yet for Christianity to surrender at this point is to sacrifice its essential basis of world community. Thus Nazism constitutes a crucial challenge to the faith of the Christian Church. This challenge makes it all the more imperative for American Christianity to mitigate the evils of racialism. The Church's first

[13]Quoted by Nathaniel Micklem, *National Socialism and the Roman Catholic Church* (Oxford, 1939), p. 23.

[14]*Mein Kampf* (Eng. tr., New York, 1939), p. 398.

[15]Cf. *ibid.*, Chap. xii.

step is to transcend racial disunity within its own household, otherwise the very nurture which it generates will be reduced to further impotency.

(c) A closely related factor to race in creating disunity in the Christian community is that of nationalism. An important element in nationalism is racialism, even though nationalism includes many other elements besides race. Nationalism is perhaps the most characteristic feature of modern civilization. It is a mode of life and thought which is intensely self-conscious and which centers in the framework of the nation-state. The contemporary nation-state is the emergent of a process which began on an extensive scale with the modern era and which has involved in its rise the interaction of many complex factors, including economic, social, political, and cultural.

No rehearsal of this historical process seems necessary for our present purpose. It is important to recognize, however, that all nation-states since the first World War have lived through a series of unprecedented crises, marking what many competent observers regard as the end of the modern era. That the present world struggle is an integral part of this disintegrative process is generally conceded. The period since 1914, in its European phase, is described by Waldo Frank as another "Thirty Years' War," during which European civilization has passed through the stages of battle, armistice, siege, and revolution.[16]

The point that should be emphasized here is that in this period the nationalist spirit asserted itself with greater force than ever, even though the internal structure of each nation was so weakened that it could do little to stabilize itself. When nations are on the brink of disaster they, like individ-

[16]*Chart for Rough Waters* (New York, 1940), p. 27.

uals, struggle to find a dynamic center of meaning; they grasp for a source of unification and redemption. That is to say, to put the idea in spiritual terms, they must get a living religion or perish. If in this situation the true supra-social center of meaningful existence has been obscured or lost, then a false or inadequate center of meaning will be chosen and made use of in the fulfilment of national destiny. It is a tragic fact that, at the very moment when national communities needed an emancipative center most, they could not find it beyond themselves. The cultural milieu of the political order was too secular to generate a living supra-social center of faith and action. What was the result? The modern nation espoused a primitive religion, the religion of nationalism. Fascism and Nazism are only extreme forms of primitive religion; other political societies, in varying degrees, depending upon the state of secularization and of social exigency, are also adherents of primitive religion.

It is of the essence of religion to seek to make disciples, and it is therefore not surprising that the religion of nationalism should be zealous in propagating itself. Nor is it surprising that this new religion should be intolerant of other faiths, including Christianity. Thus National Socialism is not content merely to preach its own way of salvation, but is jealous of all competing forms of salvation. Other faiths must not be allowed to affirm a contradictory faith, for this, as Nazi Germany well knows, would introduce tension and confusion into the "new order." In this respect National Socialism only carries to its full conclusion the logic that is implicit in the religion of nationalism. If other countries have not yet reached the stage of intolerance now practiced in Germany, it must not be assumed that their political religions do not contain the seeds of the same tendency.

The cultural situation of the West constitutes a divine judgment against the faith of the modern Church. The emergence of primitive religion is in no small measure the result of the decay and confusion of traditional religion. If primitive political religions are in a lusty state of health, it is partly due to the sickness of the conventional religions. If these new religions now challenge the right of Christianity to exist, it is partly due to the failure of the Christian Church to be true to its own faith.

That is to say, the faith of the modern Church has itself been infected with the tendency toward nationalistic religion. In its essential being the Church is one universal community, transcending all cultural and national limits. Nevertheless, the orientation of modern culture in terms of nationalism has had the tendency to orient the Christian community also in terms of a nationalist outlook, even though the Church continued to speak in universal language.

How subtly the spirit of nationalism tends to insinuate itself into the faith of the Christian community is illustrated in a statement issued by the Oxford Conference. Although the Conference warned against the danger of deifying one's own national community, it also said: "The primary call on the loyalty and service, both of the church and of the individual Christian believer, will be, as a rule, the community in which God has set him."[17] Is there not implicit in this doctrine of "primary call" the seed of the very nationalistic idolatry which the Conference condemned?

The faith of the churches which met at Oxford is now in the crucible of the second World War. In this hour what

[17]J. H. Oldham, ed., *The Oxford Conference* (Official Report, Chicago, 1937), p. 59.

Oxford called the "primary call" will assert itself with a force scarcely felt in the first World War. Oxford anticipated this tragic hour, saying: "<u>If war breaks out, then preeminently the church must manifestly be the church, still united as the one body of Christ, though the nations wherein it is planted fight one another.</u>"[18] These are courageous words, and they breathe the spirit of the Christian gospel.

Yet in the heat of conflict this seems to be one of those "impossible possibilities." In a life-and-death struggle, each of the opposing communities is compelled to live on a high plane of integration or perish. To sustain the necessary integration, each community must implicitly absolutize its cause; but that implies the necessity of ascribing absolute evil to the enemy's cause. How one can preserve the sense of Christian community under these conditions is all but impossible to conceive. In any event, the thing that can easily happen in our secular age is that the Church will corrupt its faith still further by unconditioned obedience to the "primary call." In these circumstances it will have denied its absolute center of meaning, and therefore will have undermined its basis of one community of Christian nurture.

(*d*) A final factor that is contributing to division within the community of Christian nurture is the sectarian or denominational Church. The Church as the body of Christ is one, yet history is a spectacle of many different churches, each regarding itself as a true Church, if not the only true one. Of the various reasons given for the fragmentizing of Protestant Christendom, Charles Clayton Morrison has given the latest and perhaps the most novel. "Protestantism's genius for sectarian division," says Morrison in his Lyman Beecher Lectures, "arises from its substitution of an unreal church,

[18]*Ibid.*, p. 47.

the so-called invisible church, for the real historical body of Christ."[19]

Whatever may be all the reasons for Protestant division, a sectarian Christendom is deeply disturbing to many Protestant churchmen of the twentieth century, as is indicated by the various efforts to find a way to reunion. What ultimate effect the present war may have on the ecumenical movement is uncertain, but the need for such a movement in the post-war world will be greater than ever. The difficulties will also be greater. Nevertheless, those who accept the fact that the Church is one community must seek to find a more effective way to realize that oneness within historical existence. The primary initiative will continue to rest upon the churches. "If it is true that in its deepest nature the Church is always one," says Archbishop Temple, "it is also true that today it is the so-called 'churches' rather than any forces of the secular world which prevent that unity from being manifest and effective."[20]

There is a subtle way by which the churches may unconsciously reduce their concern for a united Church. It lies in reminding themselves too uncritically that they are one already, in that they are all redeemed by one and the same God.[21] It is true, of course, that unity in this sense does not need to be created in the Church; it exists in the unity of God. On the other hand, if this fact is not made the basis of a divine judgment against our dissident historical churches, it in effect becomes an evasion of the inner contradiction between the unity of God and the disunity of the sons of God.

[19] *What Is Christianity?* p. 236.
[20] *The Second World Conference on Faith and Order,* ed. Leonard Hodgson (London, 1937), p. 19.
[21] *Cf.* Eric H. Wahlstrom, "The Kingdom of God and the Church," *Christendom,* v (1940), p. 62.

The sense of a transcendental unity can easily become a psychological substitute for the consciousness of the sin of human division.

This has particular implication for Christian nurture. For, as already indicated, the empirical community is the realistic medium of the religious education of children. Children, at least, will find it difficult to comprehend how a visibly divided Church can at one and the same time be an invisibly united one. An empirically divided Church is the one that will be most influential in molding their experience.

How divided Christendom necessarily restricts and distorts the process of Christian nurture may be easily seen by analyzing the experience of a typical child in American Protestantism. The child must enter upon churchmanship in one of our more than two hundred sects. On the empirical plane, there is no way at present to initiate the nurture of the child, outside the family, except in terms of sectarian churchmanship. On the other hand, sectarian churchmanship implicitly educates as though it were total churchmanship. This is so not merely because of inherent limitations in the child, but because of the implicit assumptions as well as the actual processes of the Church involved. Each Church assumes that it is a true Church. Even if the Church in question is committed to the "branch" theory of churchmanship, it tacitly takes itself to be a truer branch than other branches, or else it tends to weaken its own power of appeal. In respect of process, the child is received into Church membership by the use of a ritual that usually implies that he is entering, not a sectarian church but *the* Church. The educative lore used by that Church in the subsequent nurture of the child tends to give the same impression, even though a favorable reference may be occasionally made to other sectarian churches.

Thus it can hardly be denied that the educative process of sectarian Protestantism is both restrictive and ambiguous. Protestant nurture restricts the membership of the child to a sectarian branch of the Church, which at the same time tends to suggest that the child is a member of the whole Church. This is the predicament of a Protestantism which affirms that the Church is one body in Christ and yet continues to act as many parallel or competing bodies in history.

From this survey of four areas of tension, it cannot be denied that the Church itself is devoid of a radical consciousness of Christ as the supra-social center of Christian community. In this unhappy situation the empirical Church thus inevitably nurtures both children and adults in something less than one community in Jesus Christ.

4. Community of Divine Mediation

THUS FAR in the discussion of this chapter we have analyzed three distinguishing marks of the Church as a community of Christian nurture. An effort was made to show that the uniqueness of the Church as a community inheres in the fact that it emerged in history as an antecedent act of God; that it concerns itself with the ultimate fulfilment of life; and that its unifying center is Jesus Christ.

The meaning of Christian community becomes most vital, however, only when these three aspects are envisaged from the perspective of a fourth. For the fourth distinctive element of the Christian community derives from the fact of the human predicament. Apart from man's "fallen" condition, the Christian Church would not have come into being. The emergence of the Church thus bears witness to the fact that the human predicament is such that man cannot be redeemed by the resources of a purely empirical community. Why the contradictions of human existence can only be resolved by an extra-human power, we have already sought to specify. It is the Christian faith that God is that resolving power. But it is also a basic element of Christianity that God's redeeming action within the fellowship of the Church expresses itself in a particular medium. It is at this point that faith sees in the community of the Church a fourth distinctive mark. For it is the faith of the Church that Jesus Christ is the Mediator through whom God redeems men and unites them to Himself as a Christian community.

The mediative role of Jesus Christ involves two aspects, both of which are basic in the process of Christian nurture. In one aspect, the mediative action of God in Christ manifests itself as divine judgment on a world of sinful existence. This judgment, it should be recognized, is mediated not merely through the Church to the world, but also, and first of all, to the world in the Church itself. For, as already seen, the Christian community is not merely in the world, but is always to a greater or lesser degree also of the world. Therefore divine judgment through the Church must always "begin at the house of God."[1]

Divine judgment upon human sinfulness presupposes a revelation in history of the true end of human existence. It is thus the faith of the Church that the Word became flesh in Jesus Christ not only to reveal the true character of God, but also to disclose what man is in his essential nature. From the perspective of the Incarnation man is not only a sinner; he is a child of God. In the Word made flesh man sees himself not only as one who is estranged from the Kingdom of God, but also as one who may be redeemed into loving fellowship with the Father. Thus man is conscious of the

[1] I Pet. 4:17.

divine judgment only because he is aware that his conduct contradicts the law of Christ, which is the law of love. "And this is the judgment, that the light is come into the world, and men love the darkness rather than the light."[2]

Yet the fact that man knows himself, by reason of the Incarnation, to be in contradiction to the law of love, and therefore to be under judgment, does not itself constitute redemption. The human creature, to be sure, must become conscious of the fact that he is alienated from the true center of his existence and is thus under "the law of sin and of death." Unless man does know himself to be under divine judgment, there is not the slightest possibility that he will seek personal salvation. As Jesus reminded the Pharisees of his day, only the morally sick have any basis on which to desire spiritual healing. Divine judgment is therefore an indispensable preface to man's search for restoration to fellowship with the Father. But if judgment is a necessary element in the nurture of the Christian community, it does not of itself restore man to fellowship in the Kingdom of God. Out of Paul's preaching of judgment, the prisoners were indeed pricked in their hearts; but this fact only stirred them to ask what they must do to be saved. Unless Paul had had a message for his jailmates beyond that of mere judgment, his preaching would have been in vain. So with all preaching and teaching; it must transcend the plane of judgment or else fall short of its ultimate goal.[3] That is to say, it must rise to the level of "good news."

A recognition of this fact at once discloses the other aspect

[2]John 3:19.
[3]Cf. Reinhold Niebuhr, *The Nature and Destiny of Man,* Vol. 1: *Human Nature,* p. 257: "If man recognizes only judgment and knows only that his sin is discovered, he cannot rise above the despair of remorse to the hope of repentance."

of the mediating role of Christ. For in Jesus Christ the Kingdom of God comes to mankind not merely in judgment but in mercy. The ultimate character of the gospel reveals itself not in condemnation but in a love that "taketh away the sins of the world." From the perspective of divine love, the gospel is "good news," not unmitigated judgment. Thus Paul says, "There is no condemnation to them that are in Christ Jesus."[4] A God whose "wrath" against human sinfulness is sharper than a two-edged sword is yet a God who does not reckon the repentant believer's trespasses against him. This paradoxical truth eludes every canon of human reason, yet it is the wisdom of the gospel.

The gospel of the forgiving love of God in Jesus Christ is too largely neglected in the preaching and teaching of the modern Church. For well over a century liberal Protestantism has witnessed a steady dissipation of its faith at this point.[5] This has occurred, furthermore, in spite of the fact that the modern Church during this period increasingly spoke of God as "the loving heavenly Father." In fact, this sentimentalist strain, that all but captured the Church in America during the early part of the twentieth century, led to a protest by some of the more realistic liberal Protestants. They correctly saw in this tendency a dissipation of the ethical rigor of the Christian gospel. A sentimental religion took God's forgiveness for granted, as something to be expected from a loving Father.

One of the critics of this saccharine gospel was the late Arthur C. McGiffert, a distinguished liberal in the Ritschlian tradition. To conceive the gospel in terms of divine forgive-

---

[4] Rom. 8:1.

[5] For a penetrating analysis of this process in the sphere of liberal Protestantism, *see* Paul Lehmann, *Forgiveness, Decisive Issue in Protestant Thought* (New York, 1940), Chaps. II–V.

ness, he contended, is a misunderstanding.[6] According to him, the gospel is righteousness; it is ethical devotion to the Kingdom of God.[7] What the sinner thus needs "is not forgiveness," but "moral incentive and strength."[8] "Men are saved by Christ, not by being forgiven, but by being given a new purpose which itself creates new moral power."[9] It is therefore the main business of the Church to "talk to the wicked man not about forgiveness but about opportunity" for service in the Christian community.[10]

McGiffert's effort to eliminate from the gospel the element of mushy sentimentalism that marked much preaching on "love" during the first two decades of the twentieth century must be appreciated. Nevertheless, his idea of how to do this reveals a basic weakness in his own conception of the content of the gospel. He thought that the way to eradicate sentimentalism from the gospel was to reject the idea that Christianity is essentially a gospel of divine forgiveness and to construe the meaning of forgiveness primarily in terms of the forgiveness between persons. Jesus himself, McGiffert argues, had relatively little to say about divine forgiveness, whereas he had much to say about "forgiveness of one's enemies."[11] Jesus' redemptive mission, according to him, is basically twofold: first, Jesus demonstrates the true ideals of life, including the ideal of forgiving one's enemies; and second, he provides the power to fulfil life's ideal ends.[12] Thus the gospel is not divine forgiveness; it is ethical righteousness through commitment to the Christian ideal of the Kingdom of God.

This version of the gospel is very one-sided. It clearly re-

---

[6]*Christianity as History and Faith,* p. 203. *Cf.* p. 95.
[7]*Loc. cit.*
[8]*Ibid.,* p. 207.
[9]*Ibid.,* p. 208.
[10]*Loc. cit.*
[11]*Ibid.,* p. 203.
[12]*Ibid.,* p. 130.

veals the complacency of a moralistic and self-saving culture. On its terms Jesus is essentially an ethical prophet, a second Amos,[13] and a master demonstrator of the good life in the Kingdom of God. The "pressure of his [Jesus'] personality upon ours is our source of power" to live the life of loyalty in the kingdom of love.[14]

For McGiffert to hold that divine forgiveness is not the central element in the gospel shows that he did not fully perceive the self-frustrating character of human existence. That he viewed human nature romantically is a fact. It was his mature judgment, a judgment given near the end of his eminent career, "that in the minds of the best men of our age the social virtues overshadow the self-regarding virtues to a degree never seen before in Christian history."[15] Such an optimistic faith can easily dispense with the gospel of God's forgiveness. Since human goodness is progressively overcoming the world of man's inhumanity to man, ultimate victory in history of the kingdom of love is sure, given sufficient time and enough teaching about the virtues of forgiving one's enemies. Such divine forgiveness as one may require can be had, presumably, by one's forgiving those who have wronged him. Thus what one might call divine forgiveness is essentially self-forgiveness; that is, it is the concomitant of ethical good-will.

But if life be seen within the context of the true human predicament, this gospel of self-forgiveness through altruistic loving becomes a very sentimental gospel. Ironically, McGiffert's version of the gospel increased the very sentimentalism which it was intended to banish. It was itself the product of an optimistic and anthropocentric culture. It does not gauge human existence in its true character.

[13]*Ibid.*, p. 203.   [14]*Ibid.*, p. 130.   [15]*Ibid.*, p. 83.

What, then, is the human situation that calls for a more realistic gospel? The real human situation is this: man does not fulfil the law of love, even though he knows that Christ's love is normative for every life. He does not truly forgive his enemies, even though he knows that Christ in his most desperate hour said, "Father, forgive them." What, then, is the message of the gospel in this context? Is it merely a more fervent exhortation to love and to forgive? When man from the very depth of his frustrated self says, "Who shall deliver me from this death?" is it enough for the religious educator to implore him to be more loving? When man in despair asks, "Is there no balm in Gilead?" can the educator hope to resolve the moral dilemma merely by advising him to go and forgive his enemies? No! For any such approach presupposes the ability of man to resolve his dilemma within the dimensions and resources of human existence. Christianity, on the other hand, knows that man cannot resolve his own dilemma merely by human action, and it thus confronts man with a different message. It says, in the words of Paul, "God commended his own love toward us, in that, while we were yet sinners, Christ died for us."[16] In this view, man's contradiction is ultimately resolved, not by man's ability to love and to forgive, but by a Divine Mercy which, through Christ, absorbs into itself the sins of the truly repentant sinner. Thus "by grace have ye been saved through faith."[17]

[16]Rom. 5:8.   [17]Eph. 2:8.

CHAPTER SIX

RELIGIOUS FAITH. AND THE
DEMOCRATIC SCHOOL

IN CHAPTER Two it was said that modern Protestant nurture is the child of a twofold parentage—liberal religion and progressive education. Thus far, however, our discussion has concerned itself chiefly with religious nurture as determined by the nature and growth of what we have called liberal Christianity. For two reasons, though, this book should not be brought to a close without giving more definite consideration to the ethical and religious implications of the philosophy of modern or progressive education.

In the first place, one cannot fully appreciate the significance of the more leftward tendencies of liberal religious nurture as already discussed, unless one sees those trends as deriving fundamentally from an educational philosophy that grew up quite outside the historic tradition of the churches.[1] It is a significant fact that those religious educators who draw a sharp distinction between an "educational" and a "theological" approach to the theory of Christian nurture get their main support from the doctrines of modern education.[2] This then constitutes a good reason for making specific inquiry

[1] Harrison S. Elliott, *Can Religious Education Be Christian?* Chap. III.

[2] *Ibid.*, pp. 2–6.

into the religious outlook of contemporary educational thought in America.

There is, however, a second and a no less important reason for examining more definitely the basic philosophy of present-day education. It arises from the fact that there is once more a renewed effort among leaders in religious-educational thought to bring organized religion and public education into closer relations.[3] A growing number of leaders in Protestant thought believe that religion may be included as an integral aspect of the curriculum of the public school without necessarily violating the principle of the separation of Church and state. Not to incorporate religion into the curriculum, it is argued, is to distort the child's cultural heritage. Only a nation committed to an antireligious philosophy, says F. Ernest Johnson in his Rauschenbusch Lectures, can consistently exclude religion from its own schools.[4]

Yet any serious effort to incorporate organized religion into the public school will meet with vigorous resistance from a powerful school of educational thought that variously styles itself as "progressive," "experimental," or "democratic."[5] Its most distingushed exponent is, of course, John Dewey. Dewey's great work, *Democracy and Education,* published in 1916, is a classical formulation of this version of educational philosophy. Early in the present century Dewey expressed himself as being unalterably opposed to

[3]*See,* for example, Luther A. Weigle, "Public Education and Religion," *Religious Education,* xxxv (1940), pp. 67–75; W. C. Bower, "Making the Resources of Religion Available in Education," *Religious Education,* xxxvi (1941), pp. 3–8; F. E. Johnson, *The Social Gospel Re-examined,* Chap. v.

[4]*Op. cit.,* p. 182.

[5]For an excellent account of this school of thought in relation to other current educational philosophies, *see* John S. Brubacher, *Modern Philosophies of Education* (New York, 1939).

the idea of teaching religion in the public schools.[6] Organized religion, he alleged, would be a disruptive factor in the process of democratic education, not merely because of the rival activities of the different denominational groups, but also, and more especially, because of the fact that the religious faith of the churches is in definite conflict with "the positive creed of life implicit in democracy and in science."[7] Democracy itself is inherently religious, said Dewey, if one will agree to conceive "religion as natural expression of human experience."[8] Thus understood, religion is not only integral to democratic education, but incalculably important to it. In terms of natural or democratic religion, therefore, the public school should develop "the religious significance of democracy."[9] Since, however, Dewey saw little chance of getting the churches to agree to promote this sort of religion in the schools, he considered that they should not be permitted to propagate their own type of religion in them. On this basis, he reasoned, the schools of the state would be left free to promote "that type of religion which will be the fine flower of the modern spirit's achievement."[10] So far as his published views are concerned, this has remained essentially Dewey's position to the present day.

It should be said here that insofar as Dewey's version of democratic religion has been assimilated by modern religious educators, they, too, have usually opposed the introduction of the religion of the churches into the state schools on similar grounds. Thus George A. Coe recently told a national convention of religious educators that a fully democratic religion could be taught in the state schools without

[6]"Religion and Our Schools," *The Hibbert Journal*, VI (1907–1908), pp. 796–809.

[7]*Ibid.*, pp. 799–800.   [9]*Ibid.*, p. 807.
[8]*Ibid.*, p. 808.   [10]*Ibid.*, p. 809.

violating the doctrine of the separation of the Church from the taxing power.[11] Yet the present religious faiths of the churches, he contended, must be resisted by the public school. Why? Partly, of course, because the churches do not possess a unified religious tradition; but mostly because the school is not at liberty to deal with the cultural wealth of the churches in the same way that it deals with other aspects of American culture. That is to say, the schools are not free to deal with organized religion in terms of democratic or scientific method. This is because, says Coe, the religions themselves "forbid the schools to conduct such inquiry!"[12] Since therefore the state "may not—it cannot—prescribe democracy to religion," the school must refuse to teach undemocratic religion. Even so, says Coe, the public school must deny the charge of being secular, since "reverence for persons" suffuses and inspires its activities.[13]

Both Coe and Dewey thus implicitly recognize that the type of democratic school of which they speak is not really neutral in its attitude toward religion. So far as Dewey is concerned, it is clear that a positive bias in favor of a naturalistic brand of democratic religion in the schools, rather than mere neutrality, underlies his long-time opposition to having organized religion introduced into the curriculum of state education.

1. Experimentalism and the Democratic Tradition

DEWEY's bias against organized religion comes out clearly in his analysis of the nature of earlier American democracy.

[11]"The Crux of Our Problem," *Religious Education,* xxxv (1940), p. 156. *See also* "What Sort of Religion?" *International Journal of Religious Education,* xvii (1940), pp. 13–14.
[12]"The Crux of Our Problem," p. 157.
[13]*Loc. cit.*

Not long ago William H. Kilpatrick wrote: "Dewey is as truly the apostle of democracy for American education as is Thomas Jefferson for the political."[1] The truth of that statement can hardly be denied. For an examination of Dewey's long list of writings will show that he has again and again elaborated the ideals and values of democracy. It is important to recognize that <u>by democracy Dewey means</u> much more than a form of government. For him it is <u>a mode of associated living that affects all aspects of human society.</u>[2] Furthermore, a democratic mode of human relations involves also, and necessarily, a democratic mode of education.

In recent years Dewey has come to see that the roots of his democratic philosophy are to be found less in English sources than in American. His fondness for Jefferson is especially evident in his more recent exposition of democratic theory. Jefferson, he says, "was the first modern to state in human terms the principles of democracy."[3] Jefferson's democratic ethic, he holds, is "based on faith in the ability of human nature to achieve freedom for individuals accompanied with respect and regard for other persons and with social stability built on cohesion instead of coercion."[4]

Dewey accordingly finds in Jefferson's social philosophy three points of emphasis that are of enduring significance to the democratic way of life. Briefly summarized, these points are: (1) That the inherent and inalienable rights of man are the only unchangeable norms or values in a democracy, and that therefore the forms and mechanisms must

[1] "Dewey's Influence on Education," in *The Philosophy of John Dewey*, ed. Schilpp, p. 467.

[2] *See*, for instance, *The Public and Its Problems* (New York, 1927), pp. 143, 147–149.

[3] *Freedom and Culture* (New York, 1939), p. 155.

[4] *Ibid.*, p. 162.

change with the emergence of new needs and new situations; (2) that the replenishing springs of democracy reside in the free, intimate, and mutual interchange of experiences of the local community; and (3) that property rights are created by the "social pact" and therefore are modifiable in terms of the changing needs of human society.[5]

The importance of these three elements in a democracy is clearly evident. That they are also significant elements in Jefferson's social and political thought can hardly be denied. Nevertheless, they are by no means the whole of Jefferson's democratic ethic. In fact, there is reason to believe that Jefferson himself would not have considered them the heart of it. For to get at the heart of Jefferson's democratic ethic one must take into account the metaphysical framework of that ethic. Even though Jefferson was a rationalistic religious liberal, and therefore was at variance with most tenets of theological orthodoxy, he yet was unwavering in his belief that human society had its ground and goal in a divine order of reality.[6] This fundamental postulate underlies his entire structure of social philosophy. His belief in social justice, in the rights of man, and in human equality rested upon religious faith.

How firmly Jefferson believed in religion is indicated, for example, in his annual report, in 1822, to the University of

[5]*Ibid.*, pp. 157–162.

[6]While Jefferson was clearly theocentric, it yet must be admitted that his anti-Christological bias, combined with his preoccupation with the dominant ideas of the Enlightenment, gave his thought a general tendency in the direction of a secularized democratic ethic. It is by reason of this, perhaps, that Dewey and other progressive educators prefer the Jeffersonian democratic tradition to the more positively Christian strain of democracy that, in its American version, stems from New England theocratic thought, especially from such writers as Thomas Hooker and Roger Williams.

Virginia. It is commonly assumed that Jefferson had no genuine interest in religion, inasmuch as he did not give it a
place in the university of which he was the founder. That
assumption, however, is false. In reality he recognized that
religion was of the greatest importance, but because of the
intense sectarian jealousies of his time he saw no practical
means of incorporating it in the curriculum without causing
endless bickering. Nevertheless, he gave much thought to
the subject, and in 1822 he outlined a plan by which he
thought religion might be taught in separate denominational
schools on or adjacent to the university campus and thus be
accessible to all students on equal terms. In offering this plan
Jefferson said, "The relations which exist between man and
his Maker, and the duties resulting from those relations, are
the . . . most incumbent on his [the student's] study and
investigation."[7] Jefferson's hope for the maintenance of human liberty was based on faith in God. "Can the liberties
of a nation," he asks, "be thought secure when we have
removed their only firm basis, a conviction in the minds of
the people that these liberties are the gift of God?"[8]

From such statements it is clear that Jefferson's democratic
ethic was rooted in theocentric religion.[9] Yet this theocentric
frame of Jefferson's democratic philosophy is practically ignored by Dewey. To be sure, he admits that Jefferson's faith

[7]Quoted by Henry S. Randall, *The Life of Thomas Jefferson* (New
York, 1858), Vol. III, p. 468. Shortly after submitting this report,
Jefferson, in a letter to Doctor Thomas Cooper, outlined his plan for
making religion available to the students of the University. See *The
Writings of Thomas Jefferson,* Ford ed. (New York, 1892), Vol. x,
pp. 242 f.

[8]*Ibid.,* Vol. III, p. 267.

[9]For an elaboration of this aspect of Jefferson's democratic thought,
see Lula Jane Gilmer, *Some Aspects of the Ethical and Religious
Thought of Thomas Jefferson,* (Unpublished M.A. thesis, Duke University, 1937), Chaps. III–v.

in human values had some connection with a belief in "Nature—or God."[10] There is, however, no adequate recognition
or interpretation of what this involved in Jefferson's social
and political philosophy. Dewey's Jefferson is thus not the
theocentric democrat of the eighteenth century, but the
secularistic democrat of the twentieth.

A similar attitude is implicit in the democratic theory
of George S. Counts. In his vigorous and stimulating book,
The Prospects of American Democracy, he, like Dewey,
warmly applauds the democratic doctrines of Jefferson.[11] In
fact, it seems quite clear that Counts regards Jefferson as
the real Founding Father of American democracy. Yet the
rôle that religion occupied in the development and maintenance of Jefferson's democratic ethic is given no consideration. Thus one might easily conclude that Jefferson's democracy was grounded in a secular philosophy of life. The attitude of indifference which Counts displays toward religion
in relation to Jefferson's democratic philosophy he also reveals in his analysis of the forces that have given rise to
modern democratic life and thought. Consider, for example,
his excellent volume, *The Social Foundations of Education.*
In Part I, Counts surveys the basic forces in the rise of modern civilization under three headings—(1) democratic tradition, (2) natural endowment, and (3) technology. No one
would get the impression from reading this historical survey that religion had had any essential part in producing
American civilization. In five pages he discusses the origin of
the democratic ideal, but with only the barest admission that
it drew any inspiration or nourishment from religion. In
Part II Counts discusses at length—a total of 404 pages—

[10]*Freedom and Culture,* p. 164.
[11]New York, 1938, Chap. VI.

eleven cultural trends and tensions involving the family, health, recreation, science, justice, art, economy, government, etc., but he gives no comparable consideration to religion. The detailed index of the volume—covering thirteen and one-half pages—does not give a heading on religion. There is, to be sure, a topic on the church, but only two citations are given—one dealing with declining church attendance, and the other with the church as a recreational center.

Thus it appears from this brief account that both Dewey and Counts have little interest in organized religion, even when they do not actively oppose it. Furthermore, their attitude is very typical of that assumed by philosophers of progressive democratic education in general. There is reason to believe that they as a group will resist strongly the efforts of the churches to introduce religion into democratic education. Can it be that they, like Dewey, are concerned to promote a kind of democratic religion that is in fundamental conflict with the basic assumptions and ideals of Hebrew-Christian faith? In order to answer this question it will be necessary to analyze certain basic aspects of the democratic theory of progressive education.

2. *The World View of Experimental Democracy*

BY COMMON consent, the metaphysical frame of democracy has become a matter of prime concern for educational theory. Until recently metaphysical issues were spurned by progressive educators. The tide, however, has turned. Democratic theory of education, it is now admitted, must concern itself not merely with democracy as a mode of associated living, but also with democracy as a world view. Thus there are those who say that the new democracy "takes on the universality of philosophy and of religion";[1] "that it contemplates the whole of life";[2] and that it "cuts across the whole mass of our traditional beliefs and habits."[3]

That the new democracy involves a broader perspective on life is clearly revealed, for example, in the American Historical Commission's influential report on the social studies in the state schools. The frame of reference in this report assumes "that a new age of collectivism is emerging."[4] This new age, it is said, demands a democratic school that will concern itself "with all cultural interests, not with practical economic interests alone."[5] This age consequently demands a democracy whose educational doctrine will contemplate the meaning of life as a whole.[6]

What, then, is the metaphysical frame of the new democracy as conceived by the progressive educator? In seeking an answer to this question one should bear in mind the fact that not all progressive educators make explicit the ultimate basis of their democratic faith. In fact most of them confine their attention to the more concrete and practical aspects of democracy. On the other hand, the more philosophical leaders of the movement leave no uncertainty as to where they stand on the metaphysical issue. This is especially true of Dewey and of his younger disciple, John L. Childs. Inasmuch as Dewey's world view has already received some considera-

---

[1]Boyd H. Bode, *Democracy as a Way of Life* (New York, 1937), p. 51.

[2]William H. Kilpatrick, "Democracy and Social Planning—How to Unite Liberty and Security," *The Social Frontier,* IV (1938), p. 311.

[3]Bode, *op. cit.,* p. 51.

[4]*Conclusions and Recommendations, American Historical Commission on the Social Studies in the Schools* (New York, 1934), Vol. XV, p. 16.

[5]*Ibid.,* p. 41.   [6]*Ibid.,* Chaps. II, III.

tion in another context, we shall give more definite attention here to the views of Childs.

It should be noted in the beginning that Childs has recognized for a long time that the philosophy of experimentalism involves something more than method in the usual meaning of that term.[7] That it has always involved a metaphysic he has persistently maintained.[8] He thinks that the experimentalistic educator should not only admit interest in the field of metaphysics, but that he should boldly expound the metaphysical view of experimentalism. Failure to do this, he says, has already resulted in confusion through an effort to unite the procedures of progressive education with a world view that is outmoded.[9]

Childs' point of view is also significant because of another emphasis. He recognizes that experimentalism has definite implications for a philosophy of democracy.[10] These implications concern not merely what ordinarily is called the democratic process, but also, and even more significantly, the democratic world view. He realizes that democracy as a method or way of life is inherently connected with democracy as a philosophy of the universe. Thus he sees clearly that the democracy of experimentalism is not the same as the democracy of other modes of thought. The new democracy which he and other progressive educators are concerned to teach in the public school might well be called experimental democracy; that is to say, democracy as implicated in the philosophy of experimentalism.

Let us ask, then, what the world outlook of experimental

[7] One of the first to point out this fact with convincing clarity was Sidney Hook, *Metaphysics of Pragmatism* (Chicago, 1927).

[8] *Education and the Philosophy of Experimentalism* (New York, 1931), Chap. III.

[9] *Ibid.*, p. 49.   [10] *Ibid.*, pp. 30–33, 90–94.

democracy is. The quest for a world view must, says Childs, take its point of departure from "naive" or "ordinary" experience. Fundamentally, both experimentalism and democracy employ the method of experience in the search for reality. For both, ordinary experience is our only clue to the nature of reality.[11] Things are thus what they are experienced to be.[12] Reality, in other words, is not something ulterior to the world of active experience, but precisely the order of events as implicated in experience.[13] The method of experience, it is said, cuts the root of all dualistic interpretations of the world-process.

The world-process as disclosed in ordinary experience is, according to Childs, an order of indeterminate but natural events. In this order of events the ultimate traits of reality are change and novelty.[14] This "is the initial premise that permeates all of his [the experimentalist's] subsequent thought about life and education."[15] Does this natural order, then, embody anything corresponding to end or purpose? Not in the usual sense; that is, not in the sense that nature is a rational order in which some inclusive purpose is being achieved.[16] Instead, nature is a flux of incessant beginnings and endings.[17] This process of transient events, in which one event is inherently no more significant than any other, reveals no ultimate preference for any particular kind of end. The extra-human world-process is a mill that is morally

[11]*Ibid.*, p. 30.   [12]*Ibid.*, p. 92.

[13]*Ibid.*, p. 98. *Cf.* Dewey's elaboration of this general point of view in *Experience and Nature* (Second edition, New York, 1929), Chap. I, and especially pp. 4a–2.

[14]"The Meaning of the Term: Experimentalism," *Frontiers of Democracy*, VI (1940), p. 105.

[15]*Education and the Philosophy of Experimentalism*, p. 55.

[16]*Ibid.*, pp. 57–58.

[17]"Whither Progressive Education?" *Progressive Education*, XIII (1936), p. 584.

neutral toward the character of its output. In terms of experimentalist metaphysics, the forces which are hostile to human
existence are just as characteristic of reality as those which
are friendly to human welfare.[18] This complete ethical neutrality in nature is, however, strangely enough, assumed to
inspire in men the exercise of strong ethical action on behalf
of democratic ideals!

From our analysis of this aspect of Childs' thought it is
clear that his metaphysical doctrine of experimentalism has
no place for a world view that is compatible with that of
Hebrew-Christian tradition. For him, as for experimentalists
in general, nature is self-generative and self-explanatory.
On the other hand, Christian faith, as indicated in preceding
chapters of this book, sees the world of nature and of human
existence as a process of contingent events, a process which
finds its ultimate ground and goal in God. The difference
between the world view of Christian faith and that of experimental naturalism is thus a fundamental difference of metaphysical perspective. The significance of this difference for
religious nurture will appear more fully as we consider two
important consequences which follow from the naturalistic
perspective of experimentalism.

(*a*) One of the most crucial consequences arises out of
the interpretation of the emergence of human personality.
We can do little more here, however, than sketch in brief
outline some of the more basic aspects of this problem.

According to experimentalist doctrine, man emerges within
the order of natural events, and in continuity with those
events.[19] Man is, to be sure, sufficiently separate from his

[18]*Ibid.*, p. 585. *Cf.* Dewey, *The Influence of Darwin on Philosophy*
(New York, 1910), p. 44.

[19]Childs, *Education and the Philosophy of Experimentalism,* p. 52.
Cf. Dewey, *Logic,* pp. 23, 43–44.

natural environment to be able to interact with it, but the "primary fact is the unity of organism and environment."[20] Here experimentalism reveals its typical bias against all dualisms. The distinction between subject and object is made, only to be smoothed into obscurity.[21] The analysis of any organic activity, Childs says, reveals that it "is as much a function of the environment as it is a function of the organism.[22] Swimming, for example, is a function of the water as well as of the swimmer. The acquired habit of swimming thus belongs to the water no less than to the swimmer.[23] This process of interaction between man and his world is such therefore that both the human organism and the environment undergo change.[24]

The problem of the appearance of mind in the human organism has greatly concerned the experimentalist. "The experimentalist," says Childs, "ponders on the fact that man, one natural event in interaction with other natural events, has found it useful to learn how to think."[25] The experimentalist concerns himself not merely with the problem of why man has found it necessary to think, but also with the problem of what thinking signifies as to the nature of the world itself. Does the occurrence of thinking in the world throw any light on the nature of the world? More specifically, does mind in man imply mind in the universe apart from individual minds? No, says the experimentalist.[26]

One might suppose that inasmuch as the experimentalist

[20]Childs, *op. cit.*, p. 70. *Cf.* pp. 53–75.

[21]*Cf.* Dewey, *Experience and Nature,* p. 1.

[22]Childs, *op. cit.*, p. 70. *See also* Kilpatrick, *A Reconstructed Theory of the Educative Process* (Teachers College, Columbia University, 1935), p. 7; Dewey, *Logic,* p. 25.

[23]Childs, *op. cit.*, p. 71.

[24]*Ibid.*, p. 72.   [25]*Ibid.*, p. 52.   [26]*Ibid.*, p. 61.

contends that any organic activity is as much a function of the environment as it is of the organism, he would concede that an act of human intelligence at least implies something corresponding to intelligence in the extra-human world. This, however, he vigorously denies. Any such idea, the experimentalist maintains, would in effect deny "that intelligence is wholly naturalized in nature."[27] In other words, it would let the camel's nose of supernaturalism into the tent of experimentalism. Any yielding at this point would, to be sure, force the experimentalist to distinguish subject and object more sharply than a strict interpretation of the principle of continuity will allow, and this, in turn, would raise a host of thorny epistemological issues. Mind in man is therefore alleged to be the only mind there is.

This, then, raises for the experimentalist the issue of the genesis of human intelligence. How does the human mind emerge? What is the sufficient ground of human self-conscious being? Also the issue necessarily arises, what does the experimentalist mean by intelligence or mind? To get at an answer to these questions, let us recur to the idea of interaction. From the point of view of organic evolution, interaction between organism and environment occurs on different levels, ranging from the simple to the complex. On the complex or human level of interaction rational processes reveal themselves. Man the animal is continuous with the lower forms of life, yet man the thinker manifests characteristics that are uniquely different from those of the lower organisms.[28] The significant point to note here is that, according to the experimentalist, these unique mental operations "grow out of" the organic activities of the lower forms, yet so as

[27]*Ibid.*, p. 76. *Cf.* Dewey, *The Quest for Certainty*, Chap. VIII.
[28]Dewey, *Logic*, pp. 43–44.

to be not merely outgrowths.[29] How they can be truly outgrowths, and yet not be, is a problem that seems not to trouble the experimentalist, bent as he is on safeguarding his primary principle of continuity.

But assuming for the moment that rational operations really do grow out of lower organic activities, let us ask what the experimentalist signifies when he uses the term mind. Strictly speaking, he does not mean anything that denotes structure, substance, or entity. So to think of mind, he argues, tends to set mind apart as a thing-in-itself. It is this mode of defining mind that is said to be responsible for introducing into experience distinctions of subject and object, and therewith a long series of dualisms. When the experimentalist uses the term mind he thereby signifies a mode of action, a quality of behavior.[30] Thus Childs tells us that mind "is behavior that is guided by anticipated consequences."[31] Elsewhere he speaks of "behavior which is mind."[32] The same behavioristic concept of mind is implied in the doctrine that "experimental psychology observes the mind by observing the discriminatory responses or the verbal behavior of the subject."[33] In general, therefore, the experimentalist prefers to designate mind in terms of adjectives and adverbs, rather than in terms of nouns.[34]

If, then, the experimentalist means by mind a particular

[29]Ibid., pp. 18–19.
[30]Cf. Dewey, Democracy and Education, pp. 153–156.
[31]Education and the Philosophy of Experimentalism, p. 75.
[32]"The Educational Philosophy of John Dewey," in The Philosophy of John Dewey, p. 425.
[33]Edward G. Boring, et al., Psychology: A Factual Textbook (New York, 1935), p. 4. Interestingly enough, the authors tell us that their textbook, which is intended for undergraduates, is "free from the bias of metaphysical presupposition"!
[34]Cf. Dewey, Experience and Nature, p. 75.

quality of behavior, how does he explain the emergence of human mind-selves? No experimentalist has made a more careful analysis of the process of the emergence of human selfhood than the late George H. Mead. According to Mead's system of "social behaviorism," mind-selves are the product of a natural process of social interaction. A basic factor in this mind-producing process is the symbolic gesture.[35] By means of a certain gesture-signal one organism is able to evoke an appropriate response in the other, and vice versa. The simple gesture-signals of the animal become, on the human level, an infinitely complex body of symbol-meanings. When the interaction between organisms becomes sufficiently complex, and when the medium of symbol-meanings becomes sufficiently rich and directive, human mind-selves appear.[36]

It is important to recognize that, in Mead's view, the individual organism never enters into its own experience as subject, but always as object. In order therefore to become self-conscious the individual must learn to approach himself indirectly in the role of another.[37] Only as an individual incorporates in his own behavior the attitudes which another takes toward him may he become objectively aware of himself as a person. This is why Mead lays so much emphasis upon the idea of social interaction. The individual self, he says, "presupposes, and is a product of, the social process."[38] In this statement Mead recognizes that the human self is, in some sense, prior to the social process; yet he fails to clarify his position at this point. The implicit contradiction seems not to be recognized. As Robert L. Calhoun says of Mead, "He speaks with equal ease of human selves as able to

[35]*Mind, Self, and Society* (Chicago, 1934), p. 13.
[36]*Ibid.*, pp. 117–144.   [37]*Ibid.*, pp. 225–226.   [38]*Ibid.*, p. 224.

emerge only within a human society, and of distinctive human society as produced only by human selves."[39] Thus, in effect, both self and society are given an equally prior status, while at the same time there is always the tendency to explain the emergence of selfhood as wholly a product of the social process.

Mead's idea of how human selves emerge in terms of social process is also the notion that governs the thought of experimentalist educators.[40] They, like Mead, see the self as the product of interaction between organism and environment; they attach supreme importance to the role that symbol-meanings play in the creation of mind in man; and they magnify the power of culture in the shaping of human destiny. From their point of view man's emergence can be adequately accounted for within the perspective of a purely natural-social process.

(b) A second implication of experimentalism as a theory of reality involves the nature and source of values. For the experimentalist, as already indicated, nature—or "pure experience"—is, in its ultimate character, precarious and changing; it is a scene of incessant beginnings and endings. There are no unchanging forms; all events move within a universal matrix of flux. The universe is "open"!

It is against this background that the progressive educator's theory of values must be seen. He is ardent in his devotion to the values of socialized democracy. The very first step

[39]"The Dilemma of Humanitarian Modernism," in *The Christian Understanding of Man,* Vol. II: Oxford Conference Books (Chicago, 1938), p. 74.

[40]*See* Childs, *Education and the Philosophy of Experimentalism,* pp. 74; 84–86; 242; Kilpatrick, "Life, Learning, and Individuality," in *Democracy and the Curriculum,* ed. Harold Rugg (New York, 1939), pp. 352–360; Dewey, *Experience and Nature,* Chaps. VI–VII; Dewey, *Logic,* pp. 45–59.

in the new program of democratic education is, he believes, to revitalize faith in democratic values.[41] On the other hand, he contends that these democratic values must be understood in terms of the experimentalist philosophy. How, then, does this philosophy conceive values? In the first place, it holds that values do not emerge merely through the medium of experience, but that they are actually constructs of that experience. Values not only emerge within the matrix of empirical events; they are actually created by the behavior of those events. Thus the Christian claim that moral values emerge through the activity of a transcendent Being is vigorously opposed.[42]

In the second place, experimentalist philosophy emphasizes the dynamic and fluid character of values. The idea of fixed ends and standards of value is rejected. An open universe, it is said, implies that values are always changing. Dewey pointed out many years ago that "the experimental method tries to break down apparent fixities and to induce changes."[43] If one's behavior is guided by the hypothesis of change, rather than by that of fixity, one's intellectual and ethical action is said to be more creative. For change, we are told, "is associated with progress rather than with lapse and fall."[44] The idea of continuously changing values has its correlative in the idea that values are always relative to a particular context of social events. The experimentalist thus carries on a sharp and constant polemic against ethical absolutes of any kind. To treat values as though they were abso-

[41]See, for example, George S. Counts, *The Schools Can Teach Democracy* (New York, 1939), pp. 12–13.

[42]Cf. Childs, *Education and the Philosophy of Experimentalism*, pp. 38, 59–60, 93, 105; "Education and Authority," *Religious Education*, XXXIII (1938), pp. 150–152.

[43]*Reconstruction in Philosophy*, p. 113.   [44]*Ibid.*, p. 116.

lute and final is said to have the effect of producing cultural lag, and causing thereby social maladjustments.[45] It is also claimed that the absolutizing of values tends to divert the mind and effort of man from concern with the concrete events of the present world.

3. The Religious Outlook of Experimental Democracy

FROM the foregoing analysis it is clear that experimentalist philosophy implies a very definite outlook on religion. It is evident also that the kind of religion that is implied in this philosophy is in basic conflict with religion as understood by Hebrew-Christian faith. The religion of experimentalist thought may perhaps best be defined as anthropocentric religion. Three features of anthropocentric religion are especially conspicuous in current theory of progressive or democratic education.

(a) In the first place, the anthropocentric character of religion reveals itself in experimental democracy's theory of sovereignty. As already indicated, experimentalists regard nature as ultimate, self-explanatory, and self-sustaining. On this basis, a democratic ethic has no choice other than to locate sovereignty in the human order, or in some interacting process of which man is the moral source and dynamic center. Democratic religion is, on these terms, necessarily anthropocentric in its doctrine of sovereignty.

This fact is clearly understood and accepted by those democratic educators whose religious faith is framed in terms of experimentalist modes of thought. They not only teach that the ultimate source of authority in a democratic culture originates in humanity, but they contend that any other

[45]Cf. Childs, *Education and the Philosophy of Experimentalism*, pp. 65–67.

alternative involves authoritarianism. It is a mark of authoritarianism, says Childs, to teach the young "that experience cannot stand on its own foundations" without recourse to a more ultimate source of authority.[1]

On the surface this seems reasonable enough; for no intelligent educator would wisely abstract the educative process from the context of human experience. But this statement cannot be taken at face value. To get at the root of the issue that is here involved it is necessary to recall what Childs denotes by the term experience. For him, the term experience signifies not merely a mode of cognition; it signifies the character of reality as well. Taken in its ultimate character reality is only the stuff of "pure experience." From this point of view it becomes clear that Childs means to charge any religious educator with authoritarianism who teaches· the child that reality is something more than "pure experience." The religious educator may tell the child that the source of sovereignty is wholly within the flux of experience and not be an authoritarian, but if he should tell the child that this is not the case, then he is an authoritarian. In other words, if the religious educator says that the ultimate source of authority in democracy is suprahuman, he is guilty of being an authoritarian.

But why should this be so? Is it not just as authoritarian to say that the center of authority is wholly within the flux of natural-social events? No, says the experimentalist, for the latter idea represents the tested conclusions of scientific method. But does it? Has the experimentalist tested his idea that reality in its ultimate character is merely emerging events called experience? Has the experimentalist tested his

[1]"Education and Authority," *Religious Education,* xxxiii (1938), p. 152.

idea that human personality is purely the product of an interactive process between organism and environment? For him to say that he has really tested such ideas is absurd. Insofar as the experimentalist makes any such claim he is no less authoritarian than the religious fundamentalist who claims to be in possession of proven answers to problems of this sort.

Nevertheless, it hardly can be denied that the experimentalist educator operates on the assumption that he has the truth in this sphere. It is on this basis that he persistently propagates the idea that democracy is authoritarian unless it creates its own regulative standards "from within its own process" of autonomous human relations.[2] He can tolerate no sort of religious faith that is not rooted in the assumption that man is the ultimate source of sovereignty.[3] For him theocentric religion is thus absolutist, otherworldly, and a bulwark against the new democracy.[4]

(b) The religion of experimental democracy is anthropocentric also in its conception of the basis of the dignity and worth of human personality. It is a well-known fact that the experimentalist makes the value of persons the central postulate of both progressive education and the democratic faith. It is this common presupposition that inseparably links progressive education and democracy. Thus Eduard C. Lindeman writes: "Progressive Education and Democracy are to each other as roots are to plants. . . . Without education practised as a progressive discipline, there can be no democracy. If democracy disappears wholly from our earth, its

[2]Childs, *Education and the Philosophy of Experimentalism*, p. 93. *Cf.* Bode, *Progressive Education at the Crossroads*, p. 110.
[3]Childs, "Education and Authority," *op. cit.*, p. 151.
[4]*Cf.* Bode, "Democratic Education and Conflicting Culture Values," *The Social Frontier*, v (1939), p. 107.

demise will be coincident with the death of experimental or progressive education."[5]

The present crisis in American culture is inspiring vigorous effort to reaffirm the values of democracy. Nowhere is the concern for the fate of democracy more evident than among progressive educators. They believe that the democratic faith is founded upon belief in the dignity and worth of human personality.[6] For them, therefore, respect for persons constitutes the ethical pillar of democratic culture. A democracy that makes respect for persons its creative principle will, it is said, seek to develop a society that embodies the ideals of human equality, brotherhood, and freedom.[7] These ideals are thus widely proclaimed by the experimentalist. It is far from our purpose to discount the value of these ideals of equality, brotherhood, and freedom. On the contrary, we cherish them no less than the experimentalist. In fact, it is loyalty to these values that leads us to inquire whether the experimentalist has an adequate foundation on which to nourish his faith in the worth of human personal-

---

[5]"In the Face of Darkness: A Reaffirmation," *Frontiers of Democracy,* VII (1940), p. 16.

[6]"The central value in the American tradition, from which all other principles derive and to which they are subordinate, is faith in the ultimate worth and dignity of the individual." *The Social Studies in General Education: A Report of the Committee on the Function of the Social Studies in General Education of the Commission on Secondary School Curriculum of the Progressive Education Association* (New York, 1940), p. 40.

See also *Democracy and Education in the Current Crisis,* The Faculty of Teachers College, Columbia University (New York, 1940), p. 5; Counts, *The Schools Can Teach Democracy* (New York, 1939), pp. 17–18; Jesse H. Newlon, *Education for Democracy in Our Time* (New York, 1939), pp. 67–68; 94; Childs, "Dr. Bode on 'Authentic Democracy,'" *The Social Frontier,* V (1938), p. 41.

[7]Counts, *The Schools Can Teach Democracy,* p. 17. Cf. *The Prospects of American Democracy,* p. 319.

ity. On what ground, then, does he profess to believe in human worth?

A clue to the answer to this question is found in the experimentalist theory of value in general. According to experimentalism, all values lie wholly within the world of natural-social experience.[8] This denotes not merely that values are mediated through human experience; it signifies that values have no objective ground apart from human experience. "The kingdom of values," says Childs, "is within human experience."[9] Any other conception is said to be a threat to a democratic theory of value.[10] Thus the experimentalist's idea of the basis of human worth seems clear. Human worth is for him wholly intrinsic. In other words, man himself is the source and standard of his dignity and value. Human life is thus its own center of meaning. The purpose of democratic religion and democratic education alike, in this view, is to promote the "good life" within the framework of autonomous human relations.

(c) The religion of experimental democracy is also anthropocentric in its strategy of personal and social change. Faith in man as the ultimate source of individual and social remaking is implicit in the basic doctrine of experimentalism. As Dewey has frequently reminded us, experience is "an affair primarily of doing."[11] The human creature does not lie inert in the matrix of existence; he does not passively wait for something to happen. In accordance with his own dynamic nature, the human person actively experiments with selected elements of his environment. As a consequence of this experimental activity the environment undergoes certain

[8]Childs, "Education and Authority," *op. cit.,* p. 151.
[9]*Education and the Philosophy of Experimentalism,* p. 30.
[10]*Ibid.,* p. 30. *Cf.* Dewey, *A Common Faith,* p. 84.
[11]*Reconstruction of Philosophy,* p. 86.

changes, and these changes produced in the environment react in turn upon the person and his subsequent activities. "We do something to the thing, and then it does something to us in return."[12] The perception of the inner connection between doing and undergoing, between action and consequence, constitutes reflective experience. Experience involves, to be sure, both an active and a passive aspect, yet the primary aspect for the experimentalist is always lively human action.

This emphasis upon experience as an affair primarily of doing is especially congenial to the American mind. The real philosophy of the American people, Santayana has said, "is the philosophy of enterprise." Dewey's pragmatism is in his estimation little more than an explicit rendering of this philosophy, especially in its lay aspects.[13] Experimentalists themselves readily admit that there is an inner connection between their mode of philosophic thought and the pragmatic temper of American life.[14] The mastery of an expanding frontier, involving risk and uncertainty, stimulated a sense of adventure and self-sufficiency, to which industrial technology of a later period also contributed. The rapidity of change in the physical and social scene induced both a forward-looking attitude and a tendency to question all established ends and values. The preoccupation with ideas within the context of practical technics disposed Americans to view ideas primarily as instruments of problem-solving in terms of a mundane existence. All of these elements are clearly reflected, directly or indirectly, in the philosophy of experi-

[12]*Democracy and Education,* p. 163.
[13]"Dewey's Naturalistic Metaphysics," in *The Philosophy of John Dewey,* p. 248.
[14]*Cf.* Counts, *The Prospects of American Democracy,* pp. 262–265; Childs, *Education and the Philosophy of Experimentalism,* pp. 18–37.

mentalism. It is therefore no mere coincidence that a pragmatic philosophy should have flourished in the United States.

The moral and religious implications of experimentalism come to a sharp focus in the issue of the ultimate source of moral salvation. As already indicated, the object of supreme concern in experimental democracy is the human enterprise. This is the logical outgrowth of the premise that persons are the "ultimate locus of the good."[15] The moral correlative of this doctrine is supreme confidence in man as the arbiter of his own destiny. If experimentalism has any absolute at all, it is the belief that man is absolutely the captain of his soul. It is this supreme self-confidence that underlies his continuous polemic against any type of religion that bids man rely on any source of emancipation outside himself. Thus M. C. Otto, in his recent book, *The Human Enterprise,* writes: "In these critical days it is tragic to see men who mean to work for the best life attainable, sublimate their hearts' desire into a cosmic reality, mistake it for a helpful God, and so turn away from the physical world and the flesh and blood from which they must finally draw every blessing their brief and troubled existence can yield."[16]

This gospel of human self-salvation is regarded by the experimentalist as a necessary presupposition of a democratic ethic. The democratic ethic, it is said, involves faith in man's ability to manage his own affairs without the aid of extra-human forces. Thus the emergence of democracy not only implies the emancipation of man from divine sovereignty, it requires it. The voice of the people must therefore supplant the voice of God. Only on this basis, says the experimentalist, may mankind hope to realize the democratic ideal.[17]

[15]Childs, "Whither Progressive Education?," *Progressive Education* XIII (1936), p. 585.

[16]New York, 1940, p. 338.   [17]*See* Dewey, *A Common Faith,* p. 84.

At the heart of this anthropocratic ethic of democracy there are two elements. One element is romantic faith in the growing goodness of man. Edward H. Reisner, in his *Faith in an Age of Fact,* has succinctly stated the typical assumption of the experimentalist in a single sentence. "Mankind," he says, "is not a race of fallen angels, but of rising primates, come from humble beginnings and on the way to better things."[18] Even though recent events have somewhat darkened this sunny doctrine of man, it still remains an essential element in the creed of the experimentalist. He thus clings to the idea that democracy signifies the indefinite perfectibility of human society.[19]

The other element is "faith in the free play of intelligence" as the ultimate resource of personal and social change.[20] In *A Common Faith,* Dewey says that there "is such a thing as faith in intelligence becoming religious in quality."[21] The experimentalist does actually endow human reason with the aura of religion.[22] It is doubtless this fact more than anything else that inspires the experimentalist's pungent criticism of the Hebrew-Christian religion. He seems clearly to recognize that faith in human reason as ultimate moral emancipator and faith in divine redemption are fundamentally irreconcilable.

The present tendency to retreat from faith in human reason is thus a matter of grave concern to the experimentalist. He therefore appeals to democracy to become a fighting faith, to renew its faith in the method of intelligence. The task, he says, is to go forward until the method of intelligence is

[18]New York, 1937, p. III.
[19]Counts, *The Prospects of American Democracy,* p. 319.
[20]Cf. *The Social Studies in General Education: A Report of the Commission of the Progressive Education Association,* p. 40.
[21]P. 26.   [22]*A Common Faith,* p. 79.

fully operative in all social relations.[23] Although his own experimentalist creed requires that all beliefs be held tentatively, he yet fails to adhere to it himself when it comes to faith in the sovereign power of human reason. How tenaciously he clings to this faith is demonstrated by Dewey's recent affirmation: "Intelligence after millions of years of errancy has found itself as a method, and it will not be lost forever in the blackness of night."[24]

Dewey, it should be recognized, today looks askance at certain of his fellow progressive educators who in one breath profess faith in experimental method and yet in the next say, "We must be ready to meet force with superior force."[25] A few years ago he looked equally askance at those progressives who, in the early stages of the depression, urged American educators to orient their democratic philosophy in terms of the concept of the class struggle. In reference to both domestic and international policy, Dewey has frequently pointed out the inner contradiction between the use of experimental method in social change and the method of violence.[26] It can hardly be doubted that Dewey's present position reflects the logic of orthodox experimentalism. Those progressive educators who thus seek to put the new wine of conflict—whether between classes or nations—into the old bottle of experimental method will, as Dewey well knows, ultimately destroy faith in the method of "freed" intelligence. Dewey is keenly aware that experimentalism is thus on trial in the

---

[23]Dewey, *Liberalism and Social Action*, pp. 91–92.

[24]*Ibid.*, p. 93.

[25]For a notable example of the confusion against which he protests, see *Democracy and Education in the Current Crisis*, The Faculty of Teachers College, Columbia University, 1940, pp. 6, 9.

[26]*Liberalism and Social Action*, pp. 62–88; "Class Struggle and the Democratic Way," *The Social Frontier*, II (1936), pp. 241 ff.; *Education Today*, ed. Ratner, pp. 369–370.

new social scene, and he is rightly wistful that his philosophical children will consciously or unconsciously undermine faith in the rationalistic strategy of human reconstruction.[27]

From the foregoing analysis it ought to be clear that the religious faith implied in experimentalism is anthropocentric in its concept of sovereignty, in its view of the basis of human dignity and worth, and in its idea of the ultimate source of personal and social reconstruction. Thus experimentalist religion is in fundamental conflict with Hebrew-Christian faith. For Christian faith, as already indicated, envisages human society within a framework that is theocentric. It sees man from a perspective that includes the empirical natural order, but also transcends it. It expressly denies that human values can be adequately understood as to their origin, worth or destiny within the frame of a purely empirical democracy. With equal conviction it rejects the idea that the source of deliverance from sin, meaninglessness, and frustration has its center in humanity. In respect of fundamental orientation, therefore, Christian faith and experimentalist faith challenge each other. Their difference of orientation is so basic that Robert L. Calhoun seems warranted in saying they are "irreconcilable except through essential change in one or the other."[28]

This survey of experimentalist thought serves thus to bring out two things, both of which have been implicit throughout this chapter. First, it shows that the religion implicit in

[27]In this connection, *see* George Hartmann's lashing article, "Has the Progressive Education Movement Become Militarist?" *Frontiers of Democracy,* VII (1940), pp. 43–44.

[28]"The Dilemma of Humanitarian Modernism," *op. cit.,* p. 69. Calhoun's article is an extraordinarily penetrating analysis of the basic points of divergence between Christianity's doctrine of man and that of humanitarian modernism or experimentalism.

progressive democratic education is decisively at variance with that type of religious faith which underlies the doctrine of Christian nurture. Insofar, therefore, as the religious faith of experimentalism has penetrated the theory of Christian nurture it has served to distort and emasculate it. On the basis of the facts brought out in the foregoing chapters of this work, it can be seen that one.basic source of the secularization of liberal Protestant nurture is modern educational philosophy. Second, this survey reveals the fact that a paramount question now presents itself to the American people in respect of the relation of Hebrew-Christian faith to the public school. The question is not, as many have supposed, Shall the public school teach a religion? For, according to our survey, religion of a kind is already in the state school. It is that sort which we have called anthropocentric religion, and which Dewey in 1908 implied in the phrase, "the positive creed of life implicit in democracy and science." Whether or not the experimentalist educator may ever have formulated his creed in terms of commonly recognized religious ideology is beside the point. The main point is that he considers progressive education to be essentially religious. It is this assumption that either explicitly or implicitly motivates his fundamental opposition to other forms of religion, and especially those forms associated with the organized faiths, Catholic, Jewish, and Protestant. Thus the paramount question is this: What kind of religion shall the public school teach—the religion of the churches or the religion of humanistic experimentalism? Sooner or later this must become the focal point of a crucial battle. On its outcome largely hangs the fate of democratic culture in America.

INDEX

Abbott, Lyman, 34 n, 62 n
Adams, John, 156
Adger, J. B., 150 n
Adoption, 126
Agnosticism, 25
à Kempis, Thomas, 149
America, American, 1, 4, 5, 11, 18,
   19, 33, 34, 40, 55, 84, 93, 101, 116,
   122, 136, 155, 174, 176, 182, 195
American Methodism, 158
Ames, Edward Scribner, 65, 66 n, 73
Anthropocentric:
   Kingdom of God, 38–54
   Religion, 192–201
Artman, J. M., 128
Aryan, 159
Association, Religious Education,
   40, 53, 94, 112
Athearn, Walter S., 1 n
Atonement, 22–24
Aubrey, Edwin E., 31 n, 88
   Dilemma, the individual's, 86 n
   Liberalism as method, 86 n
Authoritarian, 109, 192–194
Awakening, educational, 1

Baillie, John, 114 n
Barnes, Harry Elmer, 93
Beale, Howard K., 157 n
Beaven, Albert W., 156 n
Beecher, Henry Ward, 9
Bennett, John C., 2 n, 96 n
Berdyaev, Nicholas, 67
Bergson, Henri, 49 n, 50 n
Betts, George Herbert, 101, 121
Bible, the:
   Cited, 11, 99, 106, 110
   Quoted, 42–43, 91, 98–99, 124–126,
      151–152, 158, 167, 168, 169, 172
Biracialism, 158
Bode, Boyd H., 182, 194
Boring, Edward G., 188 n
Boston University, 1 n
Bower, William C., 3 n, 128 n,
   133 n, 145, 174 n

Bible, values of the, 110
Curriculum and social relations,
   46
God, idea of, 75–76
God as a "member of the com-
   munity," 51
Kingdom of God and emerging
   values, 63
Values, relativity of, 107
Brown, William Adams, 42 n, 116
Brubacher, John S., 174 n
Brunner, Emil, 69 n, 94 n
Buckham, John W., 5 n
Burtt, Edwin A., 82 n, 127 n
Bushnell, Horace, 10, 11
   Child, nature of, 116–122
   Christology, 21–24
   Divine immanence, 5–7
   Family, organic unity of, 118
   Man, goodness of, 16
   Revivals, 117–118
   "Sacramental nurture," 119
   Science and religion, 12 n

Cadbury, Henry J., 55 n
Calhoun, Robert L., 90 n, 189–190,
   201
Calvinism, 5
Capitalism, 154–156
Carrier, Blanche, 111–112
Case, Adelaide T., 58
Case, Shirley Jackson, 18 n
Chadwick, John W., 8 n
Channing, William E., 5
   Divinity of man, 15
   Nature of Jesus, 19–21
Childs, John L.
   Democracy, religion and experi-
      mental, 192–198
   Education and authority, 192–194
   Experimentalism, metaphysic of,
      181–185
   Persons, emergence of, 185–190
   Values, nature and source of,
      190–192